50
SUCCESSFUL
HARVARD
APPLICATION
ESSAYS

50 SUCCESSFUL HARVARD APPLICATION ESSAYS

THIRD EDITION

*What Worked for Them
Can Help You Get into
the College of Your Choice*

With Analysis by the Staff of *The Harvard Crimson*

 ST. MARTIN'S GRIFFIN 🐾 NEW YORK

www.stmartins.com

Library of Congress Cataloging-in-Publication Data

50 successful harvard application essays : what worked for them can help you get into the college of your choice / with analysis by the staff of the Harvard crimson. — 3rd ed.
    p. cm.
  Includes bibliographical references.
  ISBN 978-0-312-62438-5
  1. Harvard University—Admission. 2. Exposition (Rhetoric) I. Harvard crimson. II. Title: Fifty successful Harvard application essays.
  LB2351.52.U6A13 2010
  378.1'616097446—dc22

                                                        2010018751

First Edition: July 2010

10 9 8 7 6 5 4 3 2 1

CONTENTS

Contents

IV. STORYTELLER: EXPERIENCES THAT ILLUMINATE CHARACTER

Contents

V. THROUGH THEIR EYES: FINDING YOURSELF IN OTHERS

ACKNOWLEDGMENTS

We at *The Harvard Crimson* would like to thank everyone who helped make the third edition of this book a success: Aditya Balasubramanian, the project coordinator; Clifford Marks, our managing editor; Steven Stelmach, our business manager; Peter Zhu, Esther Yi, Lauren Kiel, and June Wu, who spent countless hours putting together the final product; Matt Martz, our editor at St. Martin's Press; Katherine Boyle, our agent at Veritas Literary Agency; and all the writers who contributed their essays and the editors who wrote analyses deserve special credit for their effort.

PREFACE

Before reading over prospective work for inclusion in this book, I thought I knew what made a good college application essay. A quality choice would be well written, free of grammatical and spelling mistakes, engaging, and, above all, original. I assumed that because our pool was composed of successful Harvard application essays, all of the material would have these characteristics, and that selecting would be a matter of picking the best from the very good.

For the most part, the essays fulfilled these expectations. They were stylistically sound, well proofread, and enjoyable to read. However, after poring over more and more of the submitted work, patterns began to emerge. Tales of transformative summers spent abroad were a common trope, as were favorite home-cooked meals. By the seventieth essay or so, I could fit every essay into a category of work I had seen before.

But as topical originality faded to the background, execution came to the fore. Some of the essays clearly stood head-and-shoulders above the rest, despite their similar themes. I realized that the key was passion—the writers who cared deeply about their subject matter produced the most memorable material.

As you peruse the essays collected for this edition, I hope that you have a similar epiphany, and understand that they prove that there is nothing approaching a formula for the perfect college essay. What we have compiled in this book is a set of suggestions and remarks about some of the traits that a good essay might include. Our advice is by no means exhaustive. It is a starting point.

My only advice is to write about a topic that interests you,

Preface

whether or not you feel it is original. We read plenty of gimmicky essays that nonetheless succeeded on the strength of the writer's fervor. More often than not, enthusiasm shined through and helped separate the wheat from the chaff.

In closing, keep in mind that the essay, while important, will not make or break your application, so write without fear of failure. Best of luck!

—Maxwell L. Child
President, 136th Guard of *The Harvard Crimson*

I. INTRODUCTION:
THE ADMISSIONS ESSAY

Writing a college admissions essay is an admittedly daunting task. Most likely, you have been repeatedly told that these five hundred painstakingly crafted words must complete the intimidating mission of distinguishing yourself from the legions of other college applicants, in order to leave your own personalized mark on the admissions officers. You've probably been reminded that your essay should strike a balance between being compelling and insightful, but not too contrived. You've likely heard varying accounts of how important the admissions essay actually is: from those who swear by their writing and predict that this little essay steered them clear of the rejection pile; to others who humbly say they were probably accepted in spite of their essay. With all the academic and extracurricular work that consumes what spare time you have outside of the application process, it's almost certain that college essays aren't what you'd like to be worrying about on your weekends.

At the same time, the admissions essay can be a boon to your application if approached carefully. Each year, college admissions rates plunge as the number of applicants grows, and the size of résumés and activities lists expands. For applicants to competitive universities and Ivy League schools, having a top grade point average (GPA) along with sporting and musical prowess may not guarantee admission. The personal statement, however, is a blank slate that allows you to share and emphasize the qualities that make you stand out. It permits you to make a creative, distinctive, and even emotional appeal directly to the admissions officers. In a process dominated by test scores and statistics, the admissions essay provides a much-needed human touch. But where do you even start to find ideas for the essay, let alone write?

That's what we're here to help you do: navigate the confusing advice and vague guidance that pervades the current essay-writing process. We've provided you ten tips for writing a standout admissions essay, and we've included fifty real essays written by students who were ultimately accepted to Harvard College—with the expectation that these will give you a clearer sense of what works and what doesn't. As fellow students who have been through the college application process, we understand the questions and concerns that essay-writers often face, and in this book, we seek to provide straightforward and realistic advice that will help steer you toward success.

In the end, however, there is no single formula to writing a successful admissions essay—just as there is no single recipe for being a successful college applicant. In many cases, you're given free rein to write whatever you wish. You're the only one who can identify your greatest strengths and most debilitating weaknesses, and only you can weave that insight into a personal statement. Only you are able to articulate how different people and different experiences have molded you into the person you are today. The immense control that you have over your statement's content and style is what makes the college admissions essay so challenging to write—and incredibly revealing.

The Harvard Crimson has compiled some tried-and-true guidelines that will be helpful for writing almost any college admissions essay. Here are ten tips for you to keep in mind as you embark on the writing process:

1. *Start thinking about the essay early.* We understand that it isn't always feasible to start writing months in advance. Nevertheless, as you barrel through your senior fall, keep an eye out for potential essay topics. Read through some essays that have worked in the past to get an idea of what an admissions essay ought to look like. Consider what you're passionate about and why. Think back through your years and identify experiences, people, places, or lessons that have shaped your character and

personality. Finding an essay topic is arguably the most challenging part of the whole process, so give yourself plenty of time to think of something that you really care about. Don't be afraid to scrap ideas, even late in the process, if you come across something better—you'll find that if your topic is heartfelt, the writing will come naturally.

2. *Think strategically.* The admissions essay is your opportunity to set yourself apart, to elaborate on who you are beyond your grades, test scores, and extracurricular activities. Spend the necessary time to reflect on yourself and your experiences, and get to know your strengths and weaknesses. This will help guide you in searching for a good essay topic. When writing, don't rehash what's already evident in your résumé or application, and don't take on too much—you only have five hundred words. It's often better to delve deeply into a single experience, showing that you are an observant individual capable of honest self-reflection, than to provide a superficial exposition of interesting aspects of your life. Talk about your hobbies, play up your unusual talents or areas of expertise, or describe something formative from your past. The possibilities are endless—be creative and find something that will supplement the rest of your application well.

3. *Realize that the topic isn't everything.* Sure, some ideas—such as winning the state soccer championship—have probably been written about many, many times before you came along, and you should try to avoid those topics unless you can add something unique to the tale. Remember that your topic doesn't have to be grandiose or sweeping—sometimes, seemingly mundane experiences, such as that summer job you once had, can be the launching point into a colorful and telling insight.

Not everyone has exotic experiences or prodigious talents to showcase, but certainly every applicant has a unique and interesting background to illuminate. Creativity, thoughtful analysis, and skilled writing can make even the most routine happenings exciting. Take the time to think about your topic from various angles and figure out the best way to couch the material; showing that you can explain the "how" and the "why" of your topic is often more important than simply stating the "what."

4. *Answer the question.* If you're given a specific essay prompt, make sure your essay addresses those questions. Don't take an essay and stretch it to fit five completely different prompts; if your essay wasn't intended to answer a specific question, it becomes awkward and unconvincing. If different schools ask you why you'd like to attend their college, do your research and think through your responses carefully. Simply drafting a universal response and filling in the blanks will not demonstrate to admissions officers that you have the ability to think critically and to understand nuance. Finally, try to show that you've put some genuine thought into the essay and the question at hand. As with any good essay, use evidence, supporting facts, and examples to prove your point.

5. *Be careful with gimmicks.* Some people have successfully written poems or drawn comics for their personal statements, but they are few and far between. If you're confident that your creative efforts will turn out well, go for it. Just remember that, especially with this personal statement, execution is everything. A piece that is inauthentic most likely will not be distinctive in the way that you had hoped.

6. *Know your thesis.* As we suggested before, take the time to think through your essay topic and make sure that you know what points you're trying to make. What is the purpose of your essay? Why will an admissions officer want to read and remember your essay? What message do you want people to take away from your essay? You'll need to think through these questions in order to make sure that your message is on point and successfully delivered to the admissions officer. Knowing these answers ahead of time will also make your writing genuine, clear, and compelling. Avoid making clichéd statements and broad generalizations—everyone says they've learned from their mistakes and triumphed over adversity. Be tactful, try to write insightfully and critically, and, most of all, make sure that your message is clear.

7. *Be yourself.* The college admissions essay is a *personal* statement. Each person has his or her own writing style and tone, and essays should reflect that fluidity. It's all right to include some humor and wit, but make sure it comes naturally and isn't excessive or fabricated. While it's a good idea to have a couple of knowledgeable individuals read over your essay and give suggestions for improvement, make sure that the end product is truly satisfactory for *you.* Don't let too many people provide input, and don't let even those people you trust manhandle the content and style of your essay. This is your chance to speak directly to admissions officers and to highlight what's most distinctive about you, and you shouldn't let that opportunity be diluted by the voices of others.

8. *Be honest.* Once you settle on an essay topic, don't fall into the trap of exaggerating your experiences or the lessons

you've learned. Instead, think critically about your topic, even if it seems mundane to you, and try to understand and articulate why that experience was valuable for you—not why it might be interesting to the admissions officer who's reading your essay. Also, don't use words you don't know or wouldn't ordinarily use—that's what the SAT is supposed to test. There's nothing quite as distracting in an essay as misused words. Don't use a longer word if a shorter word captures the sentiment just as well. The admissions officers want to see that you're a clean and capable writer, and they want to get a sense of who you are and why you're distinctive. You can successfully achieve those ends without embellishing your writing or your experiences.

9. *Revise and proofread.* Write clearly and concisely, but make sure that your essay is engaging and colorful. Don't overwhelm your readers with extraneous details, and make sure to stay on point. Do not make careless grammatical or spelling errors, and do not rely on your computer's spellcheck application. Admissions officers have thousands of personal statements to read in a relatively short amount of time, so make sure your introduction is gripping. Is this an essay that you would find interesting and would want to read in your spare time? If not, keep thinking and revising. It's also a good idea to have somebody else read your essay for clarity and correctness. Let your essay sit for a few days and come back to it— you'll likely notice a lot of opportunities for editing that slipped past you the first time around. The college admissions essay is one part of your application that you have total control over, so make the most of this opportunity and keep working until you're satisfied.

I. Introduction: The Admissions Essay

10. *Relax*. Approach essays one at a time and don't let yourself get overwhelmed. Remember: The essay is only one part of your college application. Be a thoughtful and systematic writer, and when the time comes, don't be afraid to put down the pen (or walk away from the keyboard). You've done the best that you can. Give yourself a pat on the back and take a break—after all, there's more to senior year than just getting into college.

And now, on to the fun part. *The Harvard Crimson* has gathered together fifty successful Harvard admissions essays and organized them into four categories:

- The Survivor: Overcoming Challenges and Adversity
- One Among Many: Presenting a Unique Applicant
- Storyteller: Experiences that Illuminate Character
- Through Their Eyes: Finding Yourself in Others

Following each essay is a brief commentary written by a member of *The Crimson*'s staff. We hope that these examples and analysis pieces will guide and inform you as you think about your own experiences and craft your admissions essays.

Happy reading, and best of luck!

II. THE SURVIVOR: OVERCOMING CHALLENGES AND ADVERSITY

So, you want to impress the admissions officers. But chances are, you haven't saved your home from floodwaters or proved your doctors wrong after they gave you a life-altering prognosis. Or maybe you have. Writing about how you overcame adversity or failure is a common admissions essay topic, regardless of how calamitous the event was. The trick is to focus on a specific memory and to relate how that experience has shaped your character.

The following essays in this section offer a glimpse into the insecurities or hardships of the applicant's past. What makes these essays successful is the authenticity and honesty with which the writers recount their experiences and lessons learned. Whether it be a difficult move to the United States, or an incorrigible habit of speaking too fast, these essay topics can be small or even mundane, but are all human—and that's what makes these personal statements compelling. Show your readers through anecdotes, colorful details, or self-reflection how you've grown, how you've overcome a certain loss, or how you've mastered a personal weakness. The essay is your chance to show the admissions officers who you are—the *real* you.

Scott Levin—"You Speak Too Fast"

It started with my grandmother.

"You're going to have to speak more slowly, honey," she would say, interrupting me as we spoke on the phone.

I hadn't viewed my grandmother, a frail elderly woman, as a credible gauge of my intelligibility. Her hearing must be failing, I thought. Or, perhaps, her 1970s-era telephone needed to be replaced.

My father was next.

"I cannot understand a word you're saying!" he exclaimed over dinner, flecks of food flying from his mouth.

My mother would stick up for me.

"Leave the boy alone!" she would say. "I can understand him just fine! It's your hearing that's off!"

And then, one day, the dam broke.

"I'm sorry, Scotty," my mom said with a tinge of regret in her voice. "You speak too fast. I have no idea *what* you're saying."

The transition had happened over the course of months. While I had once been a child easily understood by the world, I was now a fast-talking teenager, whose language was only understood by someone from Generation Y. Among my friends, communication was easy. With adults, one needed a bilingual translator, perhaps a twentysomething.

But I remained incredulous. Adults just needed to focus more, I thought. I was speaking at a perfectly appropriate speed.

This summer, I finally began to understand my parents' struggle.

Four months ago, I traveled to Argentina to be a high school exchange student. I was excited at the prospect of attending classes entirely in Spanish; it would be my chance to attain fluency. In school, I made many Argentine friends. But speaking quickly to them seemed to be a sport. Suddenly, I was the one who was struggling to extract words from their slurred discourse.

"What do you do on the weekends?" I would ask.

"Well," a boy would start. That "well" was the windup before a long headfirst dive. "We . . . clubs . . . night . . . but . . . if . . . pizza . . . then . . . can't . . . park . . . look . . . dawn."

Suddenly, I was the one who did not speak the language. For five years I had studied Spanish. I had taken classes, read books, and tutored math students in Spanish. But none of that had prepared me to speak the language of the Argentine high school student.

I would strain. Every understood sentence was hard-fought, but, eventually, I began to sound like my grandmother: "*Vas a tener que hablar más lentamente,*" I would say. "You're going to have to speak more slowly."

The look I would receive in return was one of skepticism. Then they would ask the inevitable question: "Are you sure there is nothing wrong with your hearing?"

By the end of seven weeks, my Argentine high school friends had learned to speak slightly more slowly, and I had learned slightly more Argentine high school Spanish.

Back in California, my parents sometimes still complain that I speak too quickly. In their presence, I have slowed down as best I can because to be understood through words and their subtleties is what sets humans apart.

Only through clear communication can I connect with others. I need to hear what people say, and I need to be heard. Whether it be in my monthly newspaper column or in daily conversation, my words can have power. Perhaps words can persuade someone to stand up for an ideal, or maybe they can find the beauty in something as mundane as an old swing set.

We all go through life seeking to understand and be understood, to speak the language of the people that surround us. And sometimes, that means slowing down our speech just a little bit.

In my American high school, I see my friend Daniel Paredes, a recent immigrant from Mexico, who is struggling to learn English. He has recently been placed into mainstream English classes, and I ask him how it is going.

"My geometry class is a nightmare," he tells me in Spanish.

"Why is it so difficult?" I ask.

"Well, you wouldn't understand," Daniel says with an embarrassed tone.

"Tell me," I say sympathetically.

"It's just that, I know the English. I know the words she's saying. But she says them so fast. . . ." he trails off.

I look at Daniel and smile with commiseration.

"I understand exactly what you mean."

COMMENTARY

By tackling a flaw that the writer at first denies—speaking too fast—he describes his journey in learning to empathize. He delineates a progression from skepticism about his parents' complaints to the realization that his family has a point, and finally to self-improvement. While he blames his family at first for not understanding him, his experience in Argentina helps him commiserate with his parents' plight.

Ultimately, achieving empathy is the writer's success—but he does not drive that point home nearly as well as the importance of communication itself. While he waxes philosophical about the power of words, the writer should have used more space to explain why the ability to see through his family members' and immigrant classmate's eyes constituted such a crucial shift.

Nonetheless, this essay accomplishes a great deal in a short amount of space. Stylistically, it benefits from fluid movement through vivid pieces of dialogue. While the essay is more of a story than an argument, it is not unfocused; every sentence contributes to its overall point. The writer's direct prose style reinforces his message about empathy and the significance of communication.

—Bonnie Kavoussi

Amanda Nguyen—"Its Name Was Wheelie . . ."

Its name was Wheelie. Riding on slick, polished wheels, it was a three-foot-three-inch-high marvel of technology. Its existence and purpose formed a unique paradox—an ordinary object enabling its passengers to accomplish extraordinary things. I never thought that my seven months constrained to such a wonder could expand and change my outlook of life so drastically. Then again, I never thought I'd be bound to a wheelchair.

One Monday morning of my junior year, the subtle but persistent trill of my faithful alarm clock wrenched me awake from my dreams and signaled the start of a new day. But instead of my warm, familiar room, I found myself staring into the stark interior of a hospital. The room was decorated with colorful wires, some of which connected me to the source of my query: a heart monitor that kept beeping in error. A nurse rushed in to check the noise, and upon discovering that I was awake, bent over and clasped my hand. With an expression that read somewhere between *I am sorry* and *God, why is it during my shift that I have to be the one to break to you the news*, she informed me that my emergency heart surgery had failed. My cardiologist was much more forthright. "You are at a high risk of sudden death," she stated matter-of-factly. The failed surgery had structurally damaged my heart, and I could die at any moment until the surgeons got a chance to correct their mistakes.

That's when I met Wheelie.

I remember despising the wheelchair the first time I saw it—a tangible symbol of my newfound limitations. As time went on, less tangible but equally impairing barriers arose. I was told to stop.

Stop school. Stop activities. Stop sports. Because, as my cardiologist phrased it, "Sudden death means that life stops."

Not many people gave me much hope for maintaining my previous lifestyle. But Wheelie reminded me that while the world couldn't and wouldn't wait for me to get better, I had the choice to move forward. Just as a wheelchair must carry its passenger, no matter the weight, I learned to roll on, no matter the obstacles.

If my legs didn't feel up to moving, Wheelie helped me along.

If there was no school bell to force me to go to school, I'd force myself to wake up early anyway.

If they wouldn't teach me AP Calculus because there was no way I could possibly succeed, I'd research integrals myself.

If they said there was no way I could possibly coordinate a regional conference, I made it a point to show that I could and I would.

My efforts were not to prove my self-sufficiency. I did it as a way to get by, a method of dealing with what was supposed to be a monotonous wait for the Grim Reaper to knock on my door. In essence, by telling myself I could live, I found a way to live.

A couple successful surgeries later, Wheelie has now retired to a cozy corner of my garage. As I walk past it to join my friends for another day at school, I will never forget the sturdy little wheels that taught me the definition of persistence and hope. My physical immobility, while debilitating, led to an immeasurable shift in maturation. Wheelie didn't confine me; it gave me the freedom of another perspective on life. I saw more from three feet, three inches off the ground than I ever did standing upright.

COMMENTARY

Most college applicants probably have not experienced anything as close to imminent death as the situation portrayed in this essay.

II. The Survivor: Overcoming Challenges and Adversity

The writer's passages on attempting to maintain her past lifestyle serve as an effective vehicle for portraying her resolve in the face of adversity. The passages about her defiance while confronting a seemingly inescapable fate act as the compelling core of the essay, and she sets them up well by using the quotes from her nurse and cardiologist. While her descriptions of the different activities she engaged in during her time recovering may seem a bit self-serving, it would be difficult for any reader to fault her for a few references to achievements under such trying circumstances.

While this essay stands out for its uniquely harrowing experience, admissions officers will remember essays not for the size of the obstacle but for the applicant's experience in overcoming the obstacle. What makes this essay powerful is not so much the author's near-death experience as her determination to regain her grasp on life. The writer walks the reader through how she accomplished everyday activities that initially seemed impossible following the tragedy, and the story consequently leaves the reader with a resonating portrait of the author's resolve and character.

—Sanghyeon Park

Ashley Schneider—"Stage Fright"

Growing up in a small town has its advantages. I formed a close bond with almost all of my classmates starting before kindergarten. Everybody knows everybody else, and it is easy for parents to set up playdates. All they need to do is make a phone call, walk down the sidewalk a few blocks with a skipping, excited child in tow, then sit on a white plastic lawn chair and chat while periodically glancing up at the two kids playing happily in the sandbox. I only began to realize the downside of my town of barely one thousand people when our sixth-grade class went on a field trip to Milwaukee.

We had come to a theater to watch a theatrical interpretation of *The True Confessions of Charlotte Doyle* by Avi, which we had recently finished reading as a class. Our teacher promised that it would be exciting and fun to see the events of the book acted out on a stage with real people, and most of the class shared her enthusiasm, if not for the play then for the fact that it was our first "big" trip. We loaded into the bus early in the day, and while most chatted away the hour drive, I slept curled up by the window (I am a notorious car-sleeper). When I was startled awake by the sound of an angry horn blaring behind us, I was unpleasantly surprised by my surroundings. The buildings were too big and the cars were too many to count, but what really surprised me were the people walking on the sidewalk.

With very few exceptions, they were all black. I realized then that I had never, ever seen an African-American outside of pictures and television. As a naïve eleven-year-old, I didn't know quite what to do. When we got off the bus into a crowd of Milwaukee school children, I felt uncomfortably out of place as one of the few white students entering the theater. My friend and I tightly clutched hands, casting nervous glances around the entrance hall as more and more black people streamed through the glass double doors. We appeared to be the only school that was having such culture-shock problems. Everyone else seemed just fine with the diversity and variety that comes with a big city, but not the kids from Elkhart Lake. When we took our seats in the auditorium and the lights dimmed, I could finally relax and concentrate on the actors on stage, because we all looked black to some degree in the absence of light.

Hours later, I was happy to wake up to the familiar sight of the green streetlights lining the main street of Elkhart Lake as the bus brought us within sight of our school. I only realized much later that it is a terrible thing to be afraid of diversity, but that was what growing up in a town completely lacking in minorities did to me. Since I did not grow up surrounded by different kinds of people, the concept of race was lost on me when I first experienced it. Upon entering high school, I discovered how valuable relationships with people of other cultures are when I became good friends with an exchange student from France. I have realized that while growing up in my small town may have set me back initially, I can overcome that setback now and in the future by immersing myself in as many other cultures as I can. This is one of the many reasons attending Harvard will be an enriching and rewarding experience. If I were to repeat the field trip to Milwaukee today, I wouldn't be scared or apprehensive but rather appreciative of other ways of life and eager to learn more about the world in which I live.

COMMENTARY

In this rather daring piece, the writer tackles a hackneyed topic— diversity—from the perspective of someone who once held racial stereotypes herself. The honest nature of her essay is effective in giving the reader strong insight into who she is as a person.

Immediately, we are introduced to her small, homogeneous town, and this effectively sets the stage for her subsequent anxiety in viewing African-Americans for the first time. Even the play she watches, *The True Confessions of Charlotte Doyle*, is aptly parallel to her essay; just as Charlotte leaves her sheltered home for the rough sea, meeting people of a different socioeconomic class—sailors—the author leaves the confines of her small environment to visit the city, where she encounters people she had previously only seen in pictures and on television.

However, the writer neglects to explain how the experience molded her character, as we don't learn how or when she grew out of her race-induced fright and learned to appreciate diversity. She briefly mentions that a French exchange student transformed her outlook on diversity, but we learn close to nothing about this experience or how it showed her the value of developing relationships with people of other cultures. The reader ends the essay knowing that she is "eager to learn more about the world" without understanding why. That said, the richness of her essay lies mainly in her forthrightness. Instead of walking on eggshells, she is completely candid, and that ability to open up and be honest with herself and others makes for a compelling essay.

—Nafees Syed

NATASHA KINGSHOTT—"OVERCOMING THE FEAR OF FAILURE"

The faint whispers of gossiping spectators, players, and parents escalated as news of my defeat spread through the squash complex like an infection. "Did you see that shot . . . What a stunning upset . . ." My stomach churned and my head spun as I came to terms with reality. I buried my face in my arms, paralyzed by the loss. I was disappointed in myself for losing, embarrassed that my defeat had been so public, and angry that I had no one to blame but myself.

As my ranking climbed, so did my fear of losing. The pressure to succeed and the worry of personal and public embarrassment drove my desire to "win" in all my endeavors. Gradually, the dread of failure superseded the joy of success.

As I analyzed the match, I realized that I had hoped my opponent would make errors. Rather than playing to win, I had played not to lose, a subtle but vitally important difference in mind-set that began to seep into other aspects of my life. I hesitated to try out for a solo in a cappella, to voice a controversial opinion, or to talk to the boy I secretly admired.

Fear and passion, I realized, are two sides of the same emotion. Fear approaches a challenge with hesitation and diffidence. The potential pitfalls and difficulties generate dread and anxiety, contributing to an "Oh no!" outlook. On the other hand, passion approaches the same challenge with conviction and optimism. The promise of opportunity inspires a desire to embrace risk. I decided I needed to recapture my intrepid spirit and develop an "Oh yes!" attitude.

This more positive mind-set was soon tested as I navigated a gauntlet of testosterone in the fall of my junior year. Instead of the fishbowl arena of a competitive squash court, I found myself in the conspicuous situation of being the only girl in an all-male math class. As I advanced past a cluster of sports coats and ties, I could feel the critical stares penetrate my skin as the boys grappled with the idea that a girl had infiltrated the sacred brotherhood of Brunswick math.

The first days were awkward as I silently observed the boys, trying to find my voice, but I disciplined myself to focus on the intellectual and social benefits of the experience. Yes, it was a difficult transition, but I am a capable math student. I deserved to be there.

These positive thoughts surmounted my reservations. I was surprised to see the boys abandon their inhibitions as they yelled ridiculous answers or made animal noises in the middle of a test. They acted without anticipating or fearing the consequences of their decisions, exposing themselves every day, impervious to shame. I emulated their candor and learned from their willingness to take risks and accept the possibility of blundering. I opened myself to new opportunities, rediscovering my passion and spirit.

A few months later, I stretched into the front right corner of the squash court and lifted the ball into the air. As it sailed overhead, I was less concerned with the outcome of the point. Of greater importance was my resolve to push my abilities to the limit. I channeled my passion into a constructive emotion that inspired me to chase down my opponent's spectacular drop shot and to stay in the rally. I have come to realize that every time I compete, raise my hand in class, or attempt to hit a new note, I take a risk. I might perform at my very best but still lose.

I am no longer afraid to tackle complex math problems, but instead embrace the intellectual stimulation they provide. I confidently express my ideas, despite the chance they may be rejected.

II. The Survivor: Overcoming Challenges and Adversity

The possibility of failure still occasionally skates through my mind, but it is quickly eclipsed as I silently rejoice, *Oh Yes!*

COMMENTARY

Unlike many other applicants, the author of this essay writes about a time she failed rather than a time she succeeded. She describes the unique lesson she learned from this experience: The lesson is not that she needed to be humbled, as the reader might expect, but rather that she should be willing to take risks. She recognizes that rather than "playing to win," she had been "playing not to lose"—primarily as a result of pressures she had placed on herself to avoid failure. The essay provides insight into her thought process and shows that she is now a positive thinker who sees the benefits inherent in an experience—and in overcoming a loss.

After explaining what she learned from her squash failure, she attempts to show the reader how she turned this realization into reality. However, when the author attempts to provide evidence of her new attitude, she wanders off course when discussing how she emulated the boys in her math class. Tackling too much in too little space dilutes the strength of the essay, and the author's conclusion would have been stronger had her argument been tighter. Nevertheless, it is refreshing to read an essay that examines an old idea from a new angle, and that bears the marks of a good writer.

—Alina Voronov

Nataliya Nedzhvetskaya— "My Life"

I was born on the outskirts of Moscow, Russia, on July 11, 1991, while it was still the Soviet Union. At times my childhood memories seem more like vague dreams than concrete occurrences. In one of my earliest memories, I'm eating raspberries from our neighbor's bushes while my mother digs for potatoes. It's a warm, sunny day and the raspberries feel tart and sweet on my tongue. I am at the communal gardens about a mile from where we used to live. People have continued visiting the gardens even after it's become politically incorrect. Apparently, cucumbers and potatoes taste the same whether grown under communism or capitalism. I am four at the time.

Sometime after my fifth birthday, my father, my mother, my brother, and I left Moscow and moved to New York City. Despite both my parents having been college-educated engineers, we had a very difficult time during our first few years in the United States. Having virtually no savings and no English-speaking skills, my parents had to accept whatever jobs they could find. My father handed out flyers on the street and my mother cleaned houses. We lived on West 190th Street, deep in Washington Heights. My childhood years were a strange mixture of Russian, Hispanic, and American influences. I loved growing up in the city—the immeasurable chaos, the minute overlapping details of people's lives, the constant motion were all instrumental in shaping the person I've become. To this day, I find some sort of somber beauty in *National Geographic* editorials on inner-city environments and war-torn villages.

Living in several different places in that same neighborhood of

II. The Survivor: Overcoming Challenges and Adversity

Washington Heights, my brother and I changed schools three times in four years. My family's dynamic changed as well. I don't know if I've ever been part of a truly happy family, but I've certainly been part of an unhappy one. My parents' marriage began falling apart almost as soon as we moved to America, if not before. For the last two years of their marriage, civil conversation ceased completely. I was nine when my parents were divorced. Most children have a difficult time with divorce, dreading the very mention of the word. I was actually happier after my parents went their separate ways. It meant I could finally come into my own, rather than constantly having to worry about the problems of others. Ironically, coming into my own would take a much longer time than I had anticipated.

A few months after the divorce, my mother found an ad for an engineering job in suburban New Jersey. I had been excited for the move, relishing the idea of seeing a new place, but soon discovered the devastation of homesickness. My first year in New Jersey was one of the most miserable in my life. Though my mother came home much earlier, I was alone a greater portion of the time. In those lonely hours, I found the quiet comfort of books—truly one of the most valuable discoveries a person can make. While living in the fictional worlds of Lewis Carroll, Jules Verne, and Charlotte Brontë, I gradually adjusted to the brave, new world around me.

Problems have a tendency of staying around, changing their shape but retaining their complexity. There were still periods of difficulty in my life, such as my mother's unemployment and lack of health insurance, but I found myself ignoring these problems as best I could. Ignorance wasn't a solution but it was the best I could manage. During this time, I entered high school, attending the Academy of Allied Health and Science in Neptune, New Jersey. It was the fresh start I desperately needed. For the first time in my life, I felt I was being honest with the people around me. As a result, I started being honest with myself.

When I was a child I would stare at the sun, despite the blinding pain, just to make sure it was really there. It wasn't enough just seeing the light around me or feeling the sunshine on my skin—I needed to see it with my own eyes. In this same way, I felt I had to accept my past because I needed to know I was more than the present. Though it was painful at first, I realized that I still felt guilty for the difficulties I had encountered, as if those obstacles had somehow made me a worse person. I finally came to understand the lie I was living. If anything, overcoming those obstacles had given me resolve and empathy that made me unique. At the end of my delusion, I stared at the sun and rather than being blinded by what I saw, the past and present became strangely illuminated.

COMMENTARY

In this essay, the author undertakes the difficult task of relating the story of her entire life instead of focusing on a singular event or experience. This essay is effective, but perhaps it could have been stronger had the writer chosen to concentrate on a less expansive topic.

Students are often instructed to avoid writing about the notorious four D's—death, depression, drugs, and divorce. While this advice holds some merit, it should not deter students from addressing these issues if they truly contributed to life-altering experiences. This writer does just that by tackling an ambitious topic: the consequences of her parents' divorce.

While doing so, the author delivers her words with ease. Her style is lyrical and effortless. She addresses the joys and difficulties in her life with the same weight, neither demanding praise nor pity from the reader. She writes with an admirable straightforwardness and honesty—traits that make her both likeable and believable.

II. The Survivor: Overcoming Challenges and Adversity

Given that the topic she chose was so expansive, the writer does not directly take a long enough look at some of the turning points in her life, a key goal when writing application essays. As successful as the essay is, this is a pitfall to consider when dealing with such ambitious topics.

—Wendy Chang

Olga Zinoveva—"New Kind of Magic"

I was eleven when I got my tiny Buddha statuette. My mom explained that if I asked for one favor and rubbed his fat belly three hundred times, he would grant it. At that age, I had ceased believing that monsters lived on top of my wardrobe, but something in me still refused to abandon the possibility of fairy-tale magic.

So I rubbed his belly three hundred times, not once, but every night, always with one wish in mind: to live in America, a world full of Disney magic, where beautiful and powerful Hollywood heroes walked the streets. I must have gotten the idea of moving from my parents, who talked about it sometimes, but when we were finally on the plane to that mysterious land, it was the statuette I was thanking, not them.

But even in fairy-tale books, the protagonist never gets to the happy ending without strife. So I, too, had to overcome the language barrier, first speaking only in choppy phrases, then thinking and finally even dreaming in English. By then, I had already given up my search for magic, and even thought that this place was just another Tashkent, with a few skyscrapers here and there, and U.S. dollars instead of soms.

But as my language improved, I realized . . .

My book had two parts.

The first one was purely mechanical—a matter of practice and memorization. But the second one was intangible: I might have been thinking and writing in English, but my thought processes, experiences, and values were foreign. I had given up on the magic too early.

II. The Survivor: Overcoming Challenges and Adversity

As I understood more spoken English, I noticed that there were almost as many different opinions as people at my school, and each person debated his or her position ruthlessly. It seemed almost impudent to me: How could they argue with the teacher? But I gradually understood that here, the authority does not always hold the truth—everyone is allowed to have and voice his or her own vision of the world. And I got to have my own truth, too. When I joined my school newspaper in tenth grade, my truth gained a loud voice. This was when the idea of magic crept back to me, subtly, because such freedom was unimaginable in Uzbekistan, even if I had never dreamed about it as I did about fairies.

But my discoveries did not stop at freedom. As the years went on, America's definition as "the land of opportunity" took on a new meaning for me. There are so many choices here, most within my grasp given enough time and hard work. Here, the possibility of choosing electives both broadened and defined my interest in biology and writing, and the opportunities that colleges offered awakened my ambition to change the world. None of this would have been possible in Uzbekistan, where electives didn't exist, and everyone applied to the same college because it was the only "good" one.

But most importantly, I learned the impact that diversity had on the history of this nation, and its significance in shaping the country's policy today. I did not need to forget my experiences and traditions to be a part of this world. My connection to my native land is a big part of what makes me an individual with unique perspectives on the world and my own future.

I discovered a new kind of magic here—one that is not embodied in miracles. It is in this world's acceptance of my roots, and the freedom to grow in any direction I choose.

But is this the happy ending? I am glad to say that it is only another beginning. The next part of the story will find its protagonist on the steps of college, with a little Buddha statuette tucked safely away in her backpack.

COMMENTARY

This essay takes a prominent aspect of the author's life—her move to America and exposure to American lifestyle—and makes it part of a cohesive narrative that is both inspiring and relevant to college admissions.

After starting with a creative and intriguing opening about her Buddha statue and its potential for magic, she makes the wise decision to quickly transition into the focus of her essay: her experiences and challenges as an Uzbek native who immigrates to America. She delights in learning about the rights that most Americans take for granted, such as the opportunity to express her own opinion. The writer displays a genuine appreciation for freedom and diversity and seeks to remain true to her background while she simultaneously accepts the opportunities offered by life in America—all traits that admissions officers find appealing.

While the themes and experiences the writer discusses are all excellent ones to convey to readers, she attempts to mention so many different topics that her essay seems somewhat disjointed. While her spirit of discovery and optimism remains consistent throughout, her essay suffers from a lack of specificity. The reader ends the essay with questions about many of the details she mentions. For example, biology and writing seem like strange bedfellows—how do they relate to each other, and what exactly about her electives fostered an interest in them? Although the essay should not be a retelling of the résumé, it should also offer a little more insight into the individual and what distinguishes her experiences from those of other immigrants. Overall, the subject matter is excellent, but it would be better still with a narrower focus.

—Derrick Asiedu

Charlene Wong—"The Freedom to Be Different"

My mother returns home from work at 6:00 P.M. and begins to prepare our family dinner, just as she has for the past thirty years. Growing up, I would watch her as she stirred sun-dried goji berries and dappled *dang gui* roots into the boiling pork broth of her *bak kut teh* soup, a savory Southeast Asian dish comprising hunks of pork bones with slivers of meat that escaped the butcher's knife. Instead of conveniently following a recipe or setting a kitchen timer, she stands over the pot to periodically taste and adjust the heat setting, relying only on her ability to *agak-agak*, or approximate from memory, to make the soup just right. She knows there is an easier way; on her drive home, she passes at least two fast-food chains and a Chinese take-out restaurant. Yet, she refuses to change her routine, continuing a practice that she had established years before we emigrated from Singapore to America. Then a homemaker, she has neither adapted her practices to suit her new schedule as a working parent, nor has she accepted certain conveniences of her new life as an American. Her staunch decision to be just who she is, despite her transplant halfway around the world, has forced me to consider how I can reconcile my early youth in Singapore to my nine years spent growing up in America.

For an immigrant, the most intuitive and easiest way to become a part of one's new country is to assimilate. This was the route taken by my cousins, who when aged nine and thirteen, embraced and adopted all things "American," which for them in Georgetown, South Carolina, included drawing out their vowels to pronounce "pen" and "pin" in the same way. In contrast, my parents' dictate was to preserve who I am. I still speak with a Singaporean accent. My daily meals consist of the curries of Singaporean cuisine. I interact with fellow countrymen (not least my parents and siblings), and make an annual visit to my native island. For a long time, I struggled to find a common ground between my identification as a Singaporean and the call to be "American" as represented at school, in the media, and by my friends and neighbors. It was especially in the wake of 9/11, which occurred so close to home and so soon after I arrived in America, that I questioned whether my nonassimilation was unpatriotic, "un-American." To be sure, I fully embraced the liberty and individualism guaranteed by the Constitution, the most American of documents. But I did not know if I could dovetail the quintessential red-white-and-blue-blooded American with my heritage that is the Southeast Asian pastiche that colored Malay roots with British rule and Chinese trade. Standardized test forms told me that I was "Asian-American," but I could not comfortably append a whole culture to my identity.

Yet, as I matured and read the works of immigrant writers like Maxine Hong Kingston and Julia Alvarez, I realized that my nonassimilation is the embodiment of the most American of ideals—the freedom to be different. America is the only nation where it is tolerable, if not celebrated, for me to say certain words a different way, to crave a quarter-pound burger accompanied by *sup kambing* (mutton in spiced coconut broth), and to wear a cotton sarong instead of sweatpants at home. In France and Germany, society's message to immigrants is: If you want to live among us, you should at least appear to be like us. It is extremely telling that America has no official language (more than 170 nations do). America does not call upon her people to give up their cultural identities as soon as their right hands touch their hearts to pledge allegiance. America has never, and would never, in exchange for the privilege of being an American, ask that I revoke my Singapore citizenship, abandon the accent of my origin, or break with the traditions of my ancestors, who called themselves Cantonese, Teochew, Peranakan. To be an American, I did not have to assimilate. My cultural identity made me a part of America.

Less than a year ago, I became an American citizen as a by-product of my mother's naturalization. While my citizenship was not a conscious election on my part, as I held my navy blue passport for the first time, and saw my face and name under the "United States of America," I was struck with a deep and abiding sense of belonging. I am an American, and it feels just right.

COMMENTARY

This essay-writer impresses immediately with a vivid introductory scene (the author's mother preparing an evening meal), building to a concise statement of the conflict: namely, the struggle to reconcile the details of a Singaporean youth with the facts of American residency and nationalization. The insertion of foreign words (*dang gui*, *bak kut teh*, *agak-agak*) directly into the flow of the narrative, followed closely by their English clarifications, could easily have been cumbersome, but here it serves as an appropriate mirror of the very cultural collision that is the essay's focus.

This writer separates herself with her ability to support abstract or commonplace assertions with clever, concrete images. For instance, instead of simply telling us that the easiest path for an immigrant is assimilation (a point not intuitive for anybody unfamiliar with the immigrant experience), she gives us the example of her cousins—Singaporean expats in South Carolina. Then, instead of merely informing us that the cousins adopted a drawl, she creatively colors that information by seizing on something specific and notable: the tendency to conflate the pronunciations of "pen" and "pin." A similar instance: Where Charlene could have gotten away with the (decidedly bland) statement that "America is a melting pot" or "America tolerates a mix of ethnic identities," she gives the observation some real pizzazz: America, she writes, is a place where it's acceptable to "crave a quarter-pound burger accompanied by *sup kambing* (mutton in spiced coconut broth)." The clash of culture is elegantly embodied by a clash of cuisine in a gesture that any poet would appreciate. The writer's deftness with the material is not simply apparent in the construction of these clever verbal collisions, but largely in her ability to recognize the opposing forces at work, the richness of dual cultures, and the vivacity she alone can recognize in such different worlds, with one foot in both realms.

This isn't to say that the writer never falls down. One thing that any essay writer should be aware of is the importance of going after the right words, not the ones that sound most erudite. The pieces that sing the loudest will be the ones where the words melt off the page, leaving the reader with an unbroken series of images or impressions. It's important to think from the perspective of the admissions officer: At the end of the day, they want to see an applicant who is able to convey a soulful character, a memorable personality; therefore, make sure your writing is a vehicle toward encapsulating your identity, and not as a measure of your intelligence itself. In the end, it's easy to see through the big words and find very little behind them. Don't run the risk of being the applicant whose essay gets written off because it looks like a bad Thomas Jefferson impersonation. Leave the high English to Milton and Dryden, and focus on painting a believable picture that will last in an admissions officer's head.

—Christian Flow

ADAN ACEVEDO—"THE BROOKE RUN"

The sun woke up at around four forty in the morning every day (unless it was raining). Sometimes I woke up right as the sunlight crept into my window and pulled the little darkness I had under the covers away from me. My running shoes were always by the side of my bed, along with my shorts and a white T-shirt. As I ran out of Jesus College in the morning, I'd see Cambridge starting to rub her eyes. Men, women, and children on bikes said quick "cheers!" as they flew by. Occasionally, I would see a runner coming the opposite way and we would give each other a mutual thumbs-up. My visit to England was years ahead of schedule.

Only a few weeks prior, I had been at home, turning off my computer late at night, going to bed, and trying to decide if I was hearing gunshots or fireworks as I dozed off. I would never go out to run at five in the morning in my hometown of Lennox, California. I knew of the dangers that went with early-morning or late-night running. I have known of the gangs, drugs, and prostitution issues since I started going to school. Century Boulevard, although the exit for the Los Angeles International Airport, has an area that is infamous for being a center for prostitution. Lennox, a 1.1 square mile city, has twenty-seven graffiti gangs and fourteen much more dangerous gangs (like Lennox Trece [13] and others who steal and kill) that everyone is weary of. Teenage pregnancies come up every year, and I alone know at least fourteen or so individuals who have had children before the age of seventeen or had an abortion. Searchlights shine though my windows every once in a while, and I can't help but hope that the man or woman running will not choose to

break into my house. We have no alarm system and very few individuals in Lennox do. I have never really known the safety that
other teenagers take for granted. In a town where less than two
thousand people have graduated from high school, issues like these
do not help the academic environment of students. The odds of a
male Lennox student receiving financial aid from one of the best
high schools in the city, of not dropping out, of not giving in to gang
violence, of not giving in to the drugs or alcohol, of not fathering a
child, and of taking full advantage of his opportunities are not ex-
ceedingly good.

Yet, I was in Cambridge debating immigration, the effects of
globalization, my stance on humanitarian aid, and the right of a
beetle on the Pump Court lawn to walk into my chicken and mango
sandwich.

As sweat would begin to permeate my white T-shirt, I'd reach
the Grantchester Meadows and run along the gorgeous walking
path. I would then, after a trek of about a mile and a quarter, reach
the memorial to Rupert Brooke. Then it would hit me. The town of
Newton and Wittgenstein was just awakening. My ambition, love
for philosophy, interest in politics, and thirst for the perfect poem
or story were fed and shared by students from all over the world
there. I'd run back to Cambridge from that memorial, in eager anticipation of the day's lectures and debates in my Politics in the
Modern World class with an Oxford professor and my creative writing class with a published author. I not only had the historical town
to attest to the importance of academia, but I had the fact that I
was standing there as evidence of it. I decided I wanted to excel. I
decided I wanted something better. It had just really hit me that my
competitive nature and drive had earned me opportunities that
would leave any Lennox resident awestruck.

I drink Earl Grey tea regularly now. I walk with a different step.
I run with a smile on my face. The world's stage will soon have new

actors. I'm studying, reading, and practicing my lines so the transition into that lead role isn't too hard. However, I know I will never forget the city I came from and the issues that plague my community. Lennox gave me the few pearls it had to offer. I must give them back and with interest. I will be back in Lennox in a few years before I hit the campaign trail, go into the classroom, excel in the laboratories, or push for legislation in the United States Senate. I will be prepared and I will drive for change in my community . . . and later, the world.

COMMENTARY

This essay takes a traditional story of overcoming challenges and uses powerful and evocative descriptions to effectively convey the magnitude of the writer's achievements. The writer does an effective job of contrasting the beautiful and intellectually enriching environment of Cambridge and the tough neighborhood of Lennox where he grew up.

The writer's contrast of his two different landscapes is stark and leaves the reader impressed. The mention of "gunshots and fireworks," as well as teenage pregnancies and the lack of alarm systems, is an honest portrayal of his hometown, just as the published author and the cyclists paint a vivid portrait of England. His excitement about the learning environment in Cambridge is palpable and gives the reader a sense of how excited he would be to attend a college like Harvard, and how he would seize the many opportunities it offered for learning and intellectual development.

The main fault of the essay is that the author fails to provide context for his Cambridge experience, leaving the reader with many unanswered questions. How did he get there? Why was he there? What is this "schedule" he speaks of? Be careful not to let

your descriptions dominate the essay—helping the reader understand the point of your descriptions is often more important than
the literary acrobatics themselves. Overall, the essay's tone is candid, and the writer tells it as it is, making for an essay that is un-
deniably impressive and moving.

—Ravi Mulani

SHA JIN—"IN A PICKLE"

I woke up. The room was silent. To my shock, neither of my parents was home. I sat numbly on the floor staring into the empty room. I was alone. The mound of picture books and the pile of cassette tapes stacked against the worn sofa did little to comfort my fears, so I picked up the phone and began to punch in numbers. I was only four.

"May I help you?" a woman's voice crackled through the receiver.

I sobbed into the phone, mumbling "alone" mixed with rambles of Chinese. I was too panicked to think of the proper English words for "I've been abandoned." The woman, unable to get an address out of an incoherent, hysterical child, traced the phone number and sent a trooper to check on things. When a real policeman arrived at our apartment door, I was horrified. Dad always said that policemen existed to arrest bad children. "You wait. They'll come for you," he said grimly whenever I had been disobedient. "They'll put you in a cage, like a zoo. They feed you pickles. Lots and lots of pickles." I hated pickles.

I gaped at the shiny Houston Police Department badge on the policeman's chest and imagined him outside of my cage handing me a slimy pickle for dinner. Suddenly, Dad, who had just arrived home, saw the police sirens and ran to the door, breathless. The policeman seemed angry with Dad leaving me at home alone. As I watched the two, comprehending very little, a small bit of hope rose in my heart. For a moment, just a moment, it looked as if I wasn't going to be put in a cage and fed pickles. Dad was going to be the one eating pickles.

That night, my parents apologized and explained that they both had to work full-time, and I had to stay home alone because they couldn't afford a babysitter. After that, I began to stay home alone, following rules like "don't pick up the phone until the fifth ring," so the policeman wouldn't come back and cart me off to the "zoo."

When I grew older, my family often collected what little possessions we had, packed them into the cheapest U-Haul trailer we could rent, and drove off toward the horizon, seeking what was hopefully a better future hiding behind the sunset. I can remember listening to "Yesterday" while miles of glittery snow-covered grassland passed through the frame of the car window. I can remember a brush with frostbite in the car because the heater broke down. I can remember moments in a cold, dank Idaho motel room while Mom anxiously rubbed my feet, hoping they weren't frozen. I can remember snuggling under a blanket in the car because we couldn't afford the motel. In my childhood, I was ignorant of the true reason behind those road trips because humor, optimism, and my own innocence veiled our dire situation. Now I know that Dad was working toward his master's degree, and most of the money my parents earned went toward paying the international rate of tuition. Jobs were hard to come by, and a new place meant new opportunities.

My unforgettable experiences as a first-generation immigrant, whether it was staying home alone or sleeping in a car, have given me self-reliance, responsibility, determination, and overarching humor. I feel as if I can handle most obstacles by myself with calm tenacity, whether it's academic obstacles like AP classes or artistic obstacles like correctly phrasing a melody. These experiences have also created driving ambition and the will to succeed.

In the end, I must judge myself like those before me. My father, after arriving in the United States with only $600 in his pocket, turned what was a suicidal gamble into the American Dream. I hope to be a doer, not a dreamer, by building on what my parents began. With the drive for greatness that they have instilled in me, I will make them proud by fulfilling my potential. If an acceptance letter arrives for me in the future, the success will not be mine; it will be ours.

COMMENTARY

The "immigrant experience" typically makes for a tough college essay, usually bordering on cliché, especially given the increasingly diverse pools of college applicants today. In this particular essay, the writer combines aspects of her Chinese-American upbringing with the experience of moving around, and only later does she come to terms with why her childhood was the way it was. In making these leaps, the writer paints a portrait of her early childhood framed around a particular narrative of being left home alone and unable to make sense of why. The critical move in this essay is the transition from this narrative to an exposition on appreciating the sacrifices her parents have made and her personal motivations to succeed, given what her parents have given up for her—an insight that most applicants can draw whether they are immigrants or not, and that undergoes a refreshing treatment in this writer's piece.

As stated earlier, what often differentiates one college essay from the next is not the originality of the topic, but rather the novelty with which ideas are presented. The best essays, as this one proves, convey to the admissions officer some aspect of the writer's life in a mature and engaging sense that suggests strong reflection. This writer has clearly replayed events of her own upbringing and con- textualized them as being fundamental to her day-to-day dogma and in preparing her for the future—something any admissions board is eager to see. Make certain to focus your essay on the original ideas and conclusions you derived rather than getting bogged down in detailing the particulars of your experiences. The admissions board cares more about how this experience helped form you into the individual you are today rather than the specific details of this memory.

—Ashin Shah

MICHELLE QUACH—"UNTITLED"

The packet of published essays fell with a smug thud onto my desk. It was a collection of literary analyses on *Lord of the Flies*, and my teacher, who delighted in both aggravating the fears and stimulating the minds of his tenth-grade students, decided to read his favorite excerpts aloud to us. He promised that by studying the experts, we too could become competent writers and analyzers of literature. I listened carefully as one critic deplored readers who "subscribed to the cult of childhood innocence," and as another censured those who believed in the "romantic chimera" of mankind's essential goodness. After several essays, I sat speechless, dazzled by this show of eloquence and profundity, yet terrified as every old perception of the merits of my own writing slipped gleefully out of reach. My teacher's final proclamation was the last stab to my literary naiveté: "If you want to get an A in this class, write like that!"

The command slithered into my mind like a self-satisfied parasite and, settling in, sank its teeth into my soul. Write like that.

Up until then, I'd been fairly certain that writing was one of my talents. My affair with words began early in life. At six, I penned my first autobiography, a six-page booklet illustrated with solemn pencil drawings and held together with nine staples along the side. My teachers were Berenstain and Barrie, Cleary and Carroll, Dickens and Dahl—so even though my parents never spoke much English, I still managed to pick up an ear for the language. Writing seemed so naturally easy and creatively liberating that I simply took off, dabbling in poems and short stories, churning out even school essays with flourish and pride. I wrote the way a wild child runs: freely, ignorantly, and recklessly. My ideas spilled like water into careless paragraphs and, unrestrained by any sense of structure, sometimes sloshed ebulliently off the page.

The first time I ran into any trouble was when my eighth-grade teacher slapped a laminated hamburger on the board. The hamburger format, also known as the formulaic Jane Schaffer writing style, entered my life, and I was to live under its tyrannical rule for the next two years. My first effort, a paper on Mildred D. Taylor, resulted in choppy paragraphs that sliced up details of her life into ungraceful—though admittedly efficient—servings of concrete detail and commentary. Initially I hated and denounced the system, but gradually, in spite of myself, I absorbed its greatest asset into my writing: structure. Soon, I could pride myself on the fact that I had perfected the hamburger essay. I thought I had conquered the greatest obstacle to literary merit.

Then I found myself sitting in tenth-grade English, pummeled out of complacency by a stack of literary criticism. My teacher that year would not be satisfied with empty essays, no matter how deftly organized. Instead, he emphasized style, analysis, and use of language. The day he read us those *Lord of the Flies* analyses, I realized that I now had to strive for a more mature, insightful level of writing that I had never known existed, much less achieved, before. The thought bewildered me, but the brilliance of the published essays was unbearably enticing. My timid wonder transformed into a fanatical desire to emulate. Setting a new goal for myself, I shed my innocent misunderstandings about good writing and focused on capturing this new, more elusive quality of true excellence.

Today, the pursuit of exceptional writing still consumes me. I often sit in front of the computer for hours, typing, deleting, and retyping, trying to hit that perfect pitch with every word. Needless to say, I do not often achieve the kind of quality that I strive for, but as discouraging as this is, I can't seem to tear myself away. No matter how slow and painful the writing process is for me, in my mind I always hold the writer's craft in the highest regard. Whenever I find a piece of great writing, I sigh with rhapsodic admiration at every mot juste and genius image, every poetic description and unveiled wisdom—and I tell myself, "If you really want to be a writer, write like that!"

COMMENTARY

For starters, this is an essay that performs the very task it speaks of with great talent. This applicant focuses on the hard path toward becoming a better writer, and indeed, she displays a remarkable facility with language that, ironically, manifests itself most clearly when she describes the disillusioning recognition of her insufficiencies as a writer. For example, a particularly strong sentence is, "The command slithered into my mind like a self-satisfied parasite"—the language is precise and vivid. A simple, yet powerful, trick: Through the very strength of her writing, the applicant is able to convince admissions officers that she means it when she says she loves writing and seeks to become better at it.

Moreover, the applicant depicts her passion for writing as one that rides a constant learning curve. The author does not simply wax poetic about her love for and talent with writing, thereby leaving little room for growth—instead, this is an essay about confronting the fact that she can always become a better and richer writer, and that this is a pursuit she will gladly adopt as her own. The writer successfully conveys that she will not rest at mediocrity. Indeed, a true passion is never complacent—it strives to develop and improve, to grow into something even better than its previous state. And this is a principle the writer displays to great effect in this essay.

—Esther Yi

ADITYA BALASUBRAMANIAN—
"THE SENSITIVE ITINERANT:
CHANGES, REPERCUSSIONS, AND
DEALING WITH IT"

Background: After leaving Washington, D.C., at the end of eighth grade, I spent my ninth and tenth grade years in Hong Kong at Hong Kong International School (HKIS). Last summer, I returned to Washington for my junior year.

When a violinist changes orchestras, he often starts from scratch. The reputation he possessed in his old orchestra is gone. The other violinists are unfamiliar. And every orchestra director perceives perfect pitch differently. Whether the new pitch is too flat or sharp, the violinist must tune to the new director's pitch, lest he plays out of tune with the new group.

Returning to St. Albans School (STA) and Washington, D.C., shouldn't have been difficult. My extroversion would bring popularity. Diligence would bring academic success. Seventy-five "lost brothers" in the Class of 2008 would welcome me back with open arms.

Unfortunately, expectations proved incorrect.

After a D on my first calculus test, academic disaster loomed on the horizon. Further, rare social interaction left me miserable. Classroom enthusiasm drew eye rolling from peers. Social groups proved reluctant to accept me. But, it wasn't my peers' fault; rather, the idealist in me had expected too much. Nonetheless, they angered me. Their racist comments, which I thought them incapable of, stung.

Yet, the greatest sting came from losing my glorious Hong Kong life. Almost all 780 high school students knew me. Serving on the

II. The Survivor: Overcoming Challenges and Adversity

School Senate and writing newspaper articles everyone read blessed me with mobility between social groups few others had. I felt a part of things.

Unwilling to confront the loss of Hong Kong and my illusions, correspondence with my Hong Kong friends whenever possible temporarily appeased me. One Friday night, feeling especially escapist, I dialed my friend Kevin's number, expecting him to report all the week's occurrences. The phone rang and rang. No answer. I cried hard.

As my head hung, I saw the STA bulldog emblazoned on my T-shirt, not the HKIS dragon. Peering outside my window, I saw 8523 Pelham Road, not a picturesque skyline. I confronted the reality that D.C. was home. Deriving comfort from my friend in Hong Kong wouldn't change that.

I decided to deal with being back.

Seizing opportunities instead of lamenting the loss of a "fabled" life helped me deal with this sea change, or, more aptly, this ocean change. Smaller class sizes at a small prep school made meaningful interaction with teachers outside of class possible. In debating my English teacher about why *The O.C.* captures humanity as well as *The Scarlet Letter* and learning, mathematically, the genetic consequences of long-term sibling-sibling reproduction with my adviser, I partook in an opportunity HKIS couldn't offer. My former Spanish teacher invited me for Thanksgiving lunch and shared with me the story of her young, newly married son, a marine who recently died fighting in Iraq. The pain of changed reality in my teacher's life and her resilience in coping with it inspired me to adapt. Forging these student-teacher relationships helped me to think of life more optimistically, and my teacher's experience put my own sufferings in perspective.

In reviving a defunct Model UN team, my own experience with leadership as a process, rather than a position, began. Instead of attending Model UN conferences in Manila and Singapore, I spent time teaching underclassmen the basics of the activity and trying to educate them. Our success at the conference made me proud; although distinct from the excitement of traveling to exotic locations, teaching others successfully brought me closer to them.

Change has never been easy for me, this one especially. Nevertheless, it strengthened me for the future.

. . . The pitch was too flat, and I mourned for the old one. But in combining the old technique with the new pitch, I now play the new music and the orchestra director is happy. The other violinists offer me the occasional smile.

COMMENTARY

Overcoming change is the grand trope of college admissions essays, but this piece demonstrates not only the writer's ability to navigate through a life-changing move from Hong Kong to Washington, D.C., but his wise realization that change is often the major vehicle for progress, self-development, and maturation. The writer clearly lays out the stark differences he encountered as a result of his transcontinental move, detailing the different struggles that came his way and openly acknowledging his shortcomings and weaknesses in a new home. Instead of miring himself in the glory of his former days, the writer explains how he tackled new opportunities—a simple turnaround in the piece that gives him full liberty to do a quick rundown of his accomplishments at his new school.

Beyond the clean execution of the essay, which fulfills the basic expectations for a piece about how an individual overcame a difficult experience, it also utilizes an effective metaphor that appears at

II. The Survivor: Overcoming Challenges and Adversity

the beginning and end of the piece for a well-rounded effect. The writer does not simply discard his old life to fully embrace his new experience in America, nor does he envision himself as someone who has adapted to D.C. at the expense of his former home, but he sees himself as the embodiment of two different sets of experiences. Thereby making clear that he is not someone who simply overcomes change, but one who absorbs challenges and changes into his character to add to the wealth of experiences that already constitute his being.

—Esther Yi

III. ONE AMONG MANY: PRESENTING A UNIQUE APPLICANT

For those applicants who are serious about applying to Harvard, the desire to attend one of the most illustrious schools in the world is often well matched by an array of accomplishments, passions, and distinctions. That said, one of the more daunting aspects of the college essay is the selection of an engaging topic from those many options. As the following essays demonstrate, a compelling factor that can drive your final selection is the topic's effectiveness at setting you apart from other applicants. No matter the length of your résumé, the college essay is your one shot at putting forth your personality and character. The essay is your golden opportunity to put flesh on the bones and give passion and fire to a résumé. By successfully delivering your unique perspective and voice, you will stand out for your dynamism as well as your accomplishments.

The following essays—through a variety of methods—all possess the common denominator of showcasing the applicant's unique attitude, talent, or voice. For some, their essays' efficacy lies in the idiosyncratic subject matter addressed, from an obsession with collecting languages to a box of dress-up clothes stored under the bed. Yet, other applicants use their essays as a vehicle for demonstrating the unique and salient power of their individual perspectives; for example, there is an essay entirely constructed of pithy sentences describing the applicant that leaves no aspect of his character untouched. Whatever the method employed, these essays succeed when the applicants become real people with unique ideas and passions that they claim as their own.

Chi Zhang—"Simple Sentences"

If you give me an inch, I'll convert it to centimeters, feet, and fathoms. I'm a lover of laughter, a purveyor of puns, and an ally of academia. I look up to everything and down at nothing. My life is a tangled web of emotions, experiences, and externalities, a smorgasbord for the senses. I'm a quantitative sculpture: My height is five feet nine inches; my weight is 145 pounds; my shoe size is ten. I'm a qualitative figurine: my eyes are brown and oval; my hair is black and wavy; my body proportion is an affront to the golden ratio. I live forward but perceive the world in hindsight. I'm a natural lefty but write with my right hand. I fall prey to the passions and whims that define humanity but practice moderation. I'm Chinese by birth but American by choice. I'm a paradox, an enigmatic trope for all things ideal and inane.

Fishing in an algae-infested lake is my hobby; Rubik's Cubing is my lifestyle; memorizing the periodic table of elements is my goal; making the most of every opportunity is my purpose. I'm a pundit of trivial matters, a master baker of Sara Lee homemade cakes, and a symphonic partner to my violin. Knowledge is my true love, envy my ultimate bane, and break-dancing my primary obsession. I'm a one-time columnist for the school newspaper, a two-time Knowledge Bowl grand champion, a three-time gold medalist in the National Latin Exam, and a four-time junior middle-weight champion in finger jousting. Psychology explains my behaviors, biology determines my physical characteristics, and culture molds my social consciousness. I'm a student by day and sitcom aficionado by night. I live by the law of eccentricity (the one governing uniqueness, not

---

planetary orbits). I have sold my soul to comedy and have learned to leave my inhibitions at home. I know where Waldo is. Always. I'm averse to grammatical solecisms, prone to lisp my V's, and redolent of chlorine from swim practice. My talents take sick leaves at inopportune moments, and my true cognitive abilities kick in only after curfew. My favorite foods are detrimental to my health, and my favorite sports team isn't broadcast in North America. My search for self-identity has left me questioning fundamental tenets. But I navigate the wending traffic of life with blinkers at the ready.

I'm driven by ambition and fueled by Red Bull. My repertoire of skills is as diverse as my extensive collection of Pokémon cards. I conduct Arbuzov reactions without state-of-the-art apparatus, integrate transcendental functions without a calculator, and give stirring Latin orations to strangers without hesitation. I cringe at repetitive redundancy and avoid clichés like the plague! I am a friend to all and a foe to none. I am a vessel for emotions, hopes, and dreams. I am Chi.

COMMENTARY

With so many life-changing experiences and impressive talents under their belts, most applicants to Harvard face the obstacle of determining which subject will make for the best essay. But in this applicant's case, everything is important enough to include. In doing so, he risks generating an incoherent essay merely held together by the desire to boast about every minute detail that comprises his impressive resume. Applicants often feel obligated to share all positive aspects of themselves, but such an exercise can water down an essay into meaningless fluff. Yet, the writer largely succeeds in writing an engaging essay that utilizes everything from his amusing idiosyncrasies to his guiding passions.

III. One Among Many: Presenting a Unique Applicant

The applicant's success largely stems from his creativity in language and choice of topics. He touches upon his more obscure, almost childlike, interests—Sara Lee homemade cakes, Rubik's Cube, and Pokémon cards—and also addresses his deeper passions: his desire to push ahead into the future and his various extracurricular activities. He doesn't spend much time on each point, and thus his essay moves forward efficiently, taking the reader through a rather comprehensive journey of his serious interests and his more silly dabblings. The writer does not impose his accomplishments upon the reader and instead states what he likes and what he doesn't, simply and effectively.

Most importantly, the applicant is unafraid to reveal his shortcomings, painting a three-dimensional character that could have been easily reduced to a flat, stereotypical applicant. With admirable frankness, he concedes that his "search for self-identity has left me questioning fundamental tenets," and he is quick to acknowledge his penchant for unhealthy food and his body's nonconformity to the golden ratio. Indeed, unlike many other applicants, the writer uses the personal essay not to boast of his myriad achievements, but to give his personality a true-to-life roundness that transcends what appears on a piece of paper. He makes it clear that he doesn't assume that he's got life all figured out—rather, he is willing to "navigate" the "traffic of life with blinkers at the ready." This is an applicant who readily admits his faults and weaknesses to the service of showcasing his most compelling strength: his desire to become more than he already is.

But it's not advisable to use this applicant's approach with freewheeling abandon. One cannot deny the creativity of his essay and its efficacy in portraying an engaging character, but the repetitive, listlike nature of the essay often detracts from the power of each statement. The more varied points there are, the weaker the punch behind each point. The risk of this essay's approach is that it dilutes the writer's character by not focusing and expounding on a specific area of his life—but given this essay and its diverse array of subjects, it's hard to remain unconvinced by this applicant's ability to cohere all of the points into a persuasive character.

—Esther Yi

JESSICA HWANG—"ENDLESS FORMS MOST BEAUTIFUL"

Syllepsis. Propinquity. Villanelle. Caprice. Of all my accomplishments, I think I am most proud of being able to speak. How wonderful that my mouth can shape sounds and dispatch syllables on command. To be sure, I don't deserve all the credit, or maybe any credit, for this achievement. I owe it to millions of years of evolution pushing my vocal tract open and stuffing my head with a frontal cortex the consistency of toothpaste. I owe it to the parents and caregivers who poured a catalog of sounds into my infant ears until I started babbling back.

Perhaps the greater feat is not that I have a command of language but that language has arrived to meet me. What an epic journey it has made, evolving alongside its human carriers, spreading and mutating into countless local variants and dialects. And now I change it, too, with my willfully split infinitives and my stubborn use of the gender-neutral singular "they."

As far as I can remember, my love of language began in seventh grade, when I studied some 10,000 words for the National Spelling Bee and climbed to sixteenth place before "ginglymus" fooled me with its pretentious "y." My mom maintains that the love affair began before then, when I spelled "physiology" for a few amused grad students at the age of two. Whatever the case, words have come alive for me like organisms in so many dynamic species, each of them holding a story about ancestors I've never met.

Take "sesame," for example. Like many others, it came to English through Latin and Greek, but for millennia it traveled through Semitic languages, Babylonian and Assyrian, whose civilizations grew sesame for its oil before English even existed. Now "sesame," a survivor among so many dead species and forgotten fossils, recapitulates in three syllables the entire illustrious history of sesame cultivation west of the Indus River.

I think this is why I collect languages—English in school, Chinese at home, French for Camus's plays, and Spanish for Borges's short stories; Greek, Arabic, and Italian remain on my wish list. It's because if I am patient, each will give up its structural skeleton, its lexical ornaments, and its cultural history to me; with each one I come closer to having the right label for every situation and need. Chinese gives me *wú liáo*, for people with too much time on their hands. French gives me *décaler*, for the awful feeling of being "off," either too far forward or backward in time. Spanish provides *involucrado*, for things inextricably bound up in one another. And so on, each new word bringing me the joy of finding something I didn't know I lacked.

In *The Origin of Species*, Charles Darwin marveled at the "endless forms most beautiful and most wonderful" that he saw in the life around him. For me, words, with their seemingly infinite variety, inspire that same reverence. I should like to spend my life with words as Darwin did with his finches and barnacles and beetles, studying how linguistic species can diverge from each other, go their own way and accumulate mutations, hybridize with other populations, cross oceans and mountains, struggle to survive invasions. I think I would be happy tracing the vast network of language even as it changes constantly before us, knowing that every word I speak adds to such a breathtaking human accomplishment.

COMMENTARY

When reading the first line, an admissions officer may momentarily be offended by the string of SAT words, as every essay writer is advised not to try and impress by using big words they clearly don't understand. But the applicant takes this risk in order to surprise the reader with what she thinks is her biggest accomplishment—being able to speak—something the reader would normally take for granted.

The introduction catches the reader's interest, and it soon becomes apparent that the writer not only understands these words, but that she also admires them. Her essay stands out with the unusual analogy she makes between linguistics and evolutionary biology. While linguistic patterns are difficult to explain, she paints a picture of languages and words by referencing the stories of Darwin and his finches in *The Origin of Species*.

She uses this theme of "evolution" to tie together her future plans of studying linguistics, her knowledge of several languages and her desire to learn more. Hwang keeps the focus of the essay on herself while wandering from the history of sesame to quotes from Darwin.

Her essay is not perfect—she wastes words on the travels of sesame and mentions that she spelled "physiology" to amuse graduate students at the age of two, something that can come off as pretentious. In the end, this is a unique piece that offers readers a peek into the quirky passion of an individual. When confronted with the writer's contagious enthusiasm, it's hard to forget her.

—Alissa D'Gama

MONICA LIU—"THE SPACE BETWEEN THE NOTES"

The stucco walls of Practice Room 517 boasted dents inflicted by frustrated musicians flinging hefty volumes of classical music. This windowless cubicle had been my musical home for the past three weeks as I undertook intensive piano performance training at the International Institute for Young Musicians in Lawrence, Kansas. A Steinway grand piano held its lid open, protesting its recent demotion from concert instrument to practice room workhorse. Carefully positioning myself on the wobbly piano bench, I began to play.

I warmed up by coaxing the lilting theme of Chopin's *First Ballade* out of the grimy keyboard. The music of Chopin had always come to me naturally, for the composer's raw sentiment mirrored the creative intuition that invigorated my intellectual existence. The single-note opening of the *Ballade* was a silhouette of a narrative that sharpened as I embellished its form with floating arpeggios and cascading runs. Relishing the subtlety of the musical entrance, I unraveled this melodious mystery with the same inquisitive enthusiasm I often employed to probe scientific challenges in the laboratory. The coda was a torrent of octaves, a deluge of unapologetic passion that sparkled with spontaneity. As the tone poem evaporated in a mist of musical color, the elation of discovery lingered within me.

Impatiently dashing a droplet of sweat from my chin, I launched into Bach's D minor Concerto. As an elementary piano student, I had detested the suffocating discipline of Bach's music. Disregarding all metronomic restraints and parental admonitions, my five-year-old self had followed the beat of my personal impulses. Recently, though, I had begun to appreciate the mechanical vitality of Baroque music, marveling that the conformity of strict time signatures could nurture musical artistry. This realization has extended beyond my musical world: I now recognize that my effervescent personality, creative inclinations, and daring aspirations do have a niche in mainstream society.

As my thick hair escaped the restraints of my ponytail, the introductory phrase of Beethoven's Sonata Opus 109 enveloped my senses. A professor once commented that my interpretation of Beethoven's music was a bit too jovial: "Beethoven wrote this piece with his ear pressed to the ground to feel the vibrations from sounds he could no longer hear. Devastation cannot be conveyed with a skip and a bounce." Now, I sunk the weight of my torso into the keys, willing the spruce soundboard to resound with Beethoven's melancholy lament. The G# hammer hit the steel string with a depth of emotional ruin I had yet to encounter outside the musical world. For a moment, the universality of musical understanding transcended the enigma of human emotion.

And then, peace.

As I rose from the keyboard, my little toe rammed into a pile of musty technique books. Glancing down at my sweaty jumper and the dirty carpet of Room 517, I did not mind that my "performance attire" and "concert stage" were ill matched with the Carnegie Hall debut pianists often envisioned. This two-hour practice session required neither audience nor applause. It was simply a musical foray into raw humanity that thrived in the space between the notes.

COMMENTARY

This essay is all about the applicant, in the best way possible: Rather than badgering the reader with tales of her musical accomplishments, she uses this essay to demonstrate her relationship with music. She takes on a difficult task—describing the auditory experience of playing the piano in silent text—and achieves it masterfully. Her often succinct phrasing, combined with references to peeling stucco and a stubbed toe, creates a piece that shows intellectual rigor.

The writer sets a mood of musical expertise by using a lot of specific terminology, and then mixes in a healthy dose of more accessible description so that even the most tone-deaf reader can understand. Unusual images, like the "protesting" grand piano, give the reader insight into the applicant's unique perspective.

Yet, writing an essay that is entirely about a very specific interest is not always a sound idea. Ideally, such an essay conveys your enthusiasm for learning and ability to devote intellectual energy to a specific area of interest. There is no guarantee that the admissions officer reading your essay shares your abiding passion for being an Eagle Scout, and even the most beautifully worded essay won't convince her that knowing how to tie a square knot makes you college material. The content of your essay should convince readers of your unique personality, not merely showcase a particular skill. The content is just as—if not more—important as pretty prose. It is essential to reveal a compelling personality beneath an interest that many can boast of, and a clean writing style that many can assume.

Nevertheless, this is a well-written essay that clearly demonstrates the writer's intimate understanding of and undeniable passion for music—she is a talent, and her content makes it only too clear.

—Sarah Howland

Aditya Balasubramanian—
"Transnationalism Made Flesh"

At age six, the question of "Where are you from?" drew the automatic, effortless answer of "India." A no-brainer if ever there was one. I lived in America; that was all. No further connection.

Moving to Istanbul midway through first grade, I became attuned to my brown skin and the Indian accent of my parents, distinct from that of my peers. The strangeness of attending an American school with a British first-grade teacher named Mrs. Aldemir ("red iron" in Turkish) struck me. I attended a school separated culturally and linguistically from its surroundings. For four years, three countries punctuated my life: America at school, India at home and during the summer, and Turkey on weekends.

Returning to America to complete elementary school restored the first-grade status quo. Yet, moving to Hong Kong for the first two years of high school posed the question of where I was from in a new context. The confidence with which I answered the once obvious "Where are you from?" question disappeared as its answer grew elusive. As the classic insecurity of adolescence hit, the need to grasp my true nationality heightened. I demanded responses from my guides and mentors, who would help me with all other questions but this one. This one challenged me far beyond any other.

In *The Global Soul*, the travel writer Pico Iyer asks a Vietnamese-American woman where she is from. "America," she says. Iyer presses on, later unearthing a related anecdote. The lady confesses that once when staying in Vietnam, a hotel chambermaid asked her, "Are you one of us?" in Vietnamese. She replied with a definitive "Yes! I am one of you." The two contrasting responses capture her "state of statelessness."

Traveling to ten countries in the first two years of high school added unique complexity to my dilemma. Doesn't visiting a country, when it's not a duty-free shopping spree or an experience of cable television at a five-star hotel, but rather a cultural immersion, make someone belong to that country a little?

This past summer I spent six weeks with several global souls at the Telluride Association Summer Program at Cornell (TASP). Our seminar, International Politics on Film, could have as easily been renamed "International Politics Made Flesh." Although we often mused on the topic of where we came from, we reached no conclusions; the complexity of the question flummoxed us.

I then spent three weeks studying the Tibetan exiles living with the Dalai Lama in northern India. Although they preserve culture and religion through institutes and schools, they staunchly refuse to alienate themselves from the locals, instead coexisting fraternally. Some I met were as interested in whether or not the famous Bollywood actor Sanjay Dutt would get bailed out of jail as they were in news from Tibet. Several were born in India. The Tibetan refugees have more diplomatic missions in foreign lands than some countries have embassies! Where are the Tibetans, with no nation or citizenship, from?

Iyer makes no conclusions on the transnational identity, choosing, like most global souls, to celebrate it rather than define it. That's a good policy.

Nationality allows easy identification, providing a way to connect with similar people. But through my life I've seen that as enthusiastic as people are to bond with others of the same nationality, they are reluctant to share this relationship with people of different nations. My Chinese friends' parents have mainly Chinese friends, and many view foreigners with scorn. My Indian friends' families have mainly Indian friends, and they want their kids to marry Indian, as if to protect a dying breed.

So I've abandoned the question of where I come from as a mark of insecurity of those who feel the need to erect human barriers. Having roots like a banyan tree and no nation to concretely come from has forced interaction with everyone I meet. That's why I loved the kids at TASP and could understand the Tibetans' desire to integrate with the locals; they connect indiscriminately, establishing the human condition itself as a common denominator. And that's been the story of my life. My yearning for constant human connection defines me better than any myopic notion of nationality ever will.

COMMENTARY

The writing in this essay is not artful or elegant. Rather it succeeds on the strength of its content. One thing to keep in mind as you write your admissions piece—particularly if you don't feel like the strength of your writing alone will carry you over the bar—is to focus on an experience you can claim that nobody else can. Bear in mind that the admissions team prides itself on piecing together an entering class with as many dimensions as possible, and that it often boasts that its incoming freshmen will learn more from each other than they ever will in the classroom. It's up to you, then, to sell what fresh dimension you bring, and how that dimension will contribute to the class at large. Your fresh dimension could be something extremely narrow: like that one time in high school you tried to yo-yo while unicycling, or it could be a more general fact of your upbringing or life. What matters most of all is that you justify its consequence to the 1,600 others that will count themselves your classmates for the four years that you are on campus. How will the people around you be affected by the piece of the diversity puzzle you bring? How will they learn and benefit from the experience that you bring to the picture?

In this particular essay, we are informed that the writer has visited "ten countries in the first two years of high school," and has been a resident of at least three of them—something that adds complexity to issues of nationality. And indeed, this is unique: Very few of the thousands of applicants will be able to claim such extensive international experience.

Now, for the coup de grace: How will the applicant marshal the wealth of international experience in a way that will make him an asset to his class? Well, in the first place, he has not only had experience of these countries, but has evidently used his experiences as a platform upon which to consider some rather complex questions. The problem of nationality and identification would be enough to keep a fleet of doctoral students going for a good while, and this writer hasn't shied away from it in his life or this essay. Beyond that, there is also a nice little attestation of how his ruminations on nationality have made him a more open person, somebody who yearns for "constant human connection" of all kinds and colors and creeds. That is the sort of open attitude that many colleges are looking for.

—Christian Flow

DANIEL HERZ-ROIPHE—"HARVARD SUPPLEMENT ESSAY"

Every year at Thanksgiving, my mother reads the same passage from *Charlotte's Web*, and every year it makes her cry. I am not predisposed to crying. However, the ending of *Charlotte's Web*, with its simple declarative sentences describing "the passage of swallows, the nearness of rats, the sameness of sheep, the love of spiders, the smell of manure, and the glory of everything," conjures up more emotion in me than practically any other work of literature. It is inextricably linked with memories of childhood Thanksgivings, when my extended family, with its secular humanist bent, gave thanks through prose rather than through prayer. While Judaism holds some sway, Literature is the true religion of choice at my family functions. My relatives, a bunch of writers, lawyers, and psychoanalysts, are all creators or interpreters of words, so perhaps it was inevitable that I am captivated by language myself.

Charlotte, E. B. White's arachnid heroine, is fully aware of the power of words. She uses her web to proclaim Wilbur, "Some Pig," and, miraculously, the previously unremarkable animal becomes just that. Similarly, she manages to make her friend "terrific," "radiant," and even "humble" through the words of her web. While the self-effacing Charlotte attributes the success of her ploy to man's gullibility, claiming, "People believe almost anything they see in print," there is clearly more at work than simple deception. When farmers from miles around gather to gawk at the seemingly phenomenal pig, they are not truly being fooled, for Wilbur successively takes on each of the attributes that are ascribed to him in the spider's web. Life conforms to Charlotte's writing. The consummate author, she uses her words to forge a new reality. She belongs to a tradition of creation through language that stretches back as far as the Book of Genesis, in which the entire universe is brought into existence through the utterance of words, or the New Testament, where language and deity are explicitly equated: "In the beginning there was the Word . . . and the Word was God" (John, 1-1).

Charlotte is no goddess. She is only a spider, who dies alone in her final act of creation. But through her use of language, she becomes not only anthropomorphic, but theomorphic as well. She is a model of simple and efficient style. Over the course of the novel, Charlotte writes only five words, but succeeds in fundamentally altering reality.

Like Charlotte, I am a lover of words. Nearly every passion I have—politics, history, English, debate, Model UN, French—is centered on the word. Words are the means by which humans categorize and take possession of the world, and relate to one another. Words allow me to comprehend reality instead of merely experiencing it.

E. B. White ends his novel with a beautifully simple pronouncement: "It is not often someone comes along who is a true friend and a good writer. Charlotte was both." I can only hope that one day someone will say the same thing about me.

COMMENTARY

Personal yet universal—that is the reason this essay works so well. First, the applicant begins with an anecdote about his family that draws the reader in on an emotional level. Then he transitions to a topic that most readers are familiar with: the popular book *Charlotte's Web*. After a brief analysis of the story, the writer concludes by venturing back into the personal realm. He does a good job of intertwining the book and its contents into the larger importance of words in his life, and his ability to recognize how a small family activity ties into a larger passion is impressive.

When writing an essay referencing a story, one must be careful not to let plot summary overshadow the personal connection to the text and its themes. Maximum word counts only allow for so much space, and a summary can quickly become unwieldy. From a purely visual perspective, the essay looks heavier in the summary-laden first half than in the more analytical second section. A few more sentences about how the applicant is a lover of words would have allowed the reader a longer look into why he chose to discuss this text in his essay.

Those two alterations, however, are minor in nature. The most important thing that this applicant does in this essay is show that he aspires to be not only a smart and capable writer, but also a person with whom another student would want to live and be friends.

—Alix Olian

ADRIENNE LEE—"JOURNEYS FROM THE DRESS-UP BOX"

I have had an illustrious past. I have been a pirate, a knight, and a Native American princess. I have traveled to many lands, done great deeds, and witnessed incredible sights, while still eating home-cooked meals and sleeping in my own bed.

The secret to my amazing feat? Excellent travel attire . . . a motley crew of scarves, ethnic clothing, and strange items not fashionable since the '80s—relics from my mother's closet. To me, every slip of cloth was a passage to a new identity. I donned a silk tunic belted with a scarf and I was Artemis, Goddess of the Hunt; a long flowery skirt and I was an English lady sitting down to tea; a too-large checkered dress and I was a peasant girl diligently tending to the farm. I eventually recruited my younger brother to participate in my elaborate stories, which were not bound by time or place. Together we operated a ranch on the Mexican frontier, explored our steep hillside backyard as Lewis and Clark, and operated a space-ship headed for another galaxy. Scarves became turbans, shawls, and saris, depending on what the story called for. Dressing up was no mere play activity to me; it was serious business.

The dress-up clothes now lie under my bed in a large storage box. Sometime during middle school I stopped taking them out. My costume-fueled adventures gave way to schoolwork, swimming, and extracurricular activities. I channeled my creative energy into school projects, producing artistic masterpieces that greatly exceeded the general guidelines of "book report" or "illustrated timeline."

During a two-week stint in a Shakespeare performance camp, I discovered acting as a means of telling stories. Infected with the acting bug, I pursued theatrical opportunities with relish, eventually landing the lead in my school's winter play. On the stage, I was no longer a college-bound Asian-American girl. I was a poor, tough-talking truant living in the midst of the Great Depression. I feared the hopelessness that enveloped my world, but I dreamed of escaping my rural town and finding a better life.

My imagined journeys into worlds outside my own also developed into a genuine love of studying history. I found that every time period had its great themes and fascinating events and that every place had a unique story. I devoured tales from ancient Egypt, classical Greece, medieval China, and modern Europe, with their complex plots winding through wars, famines, epidemics, and revolutions. Dynamic characters and high drama—history is truly the longest novel ever written. Today's stories parallel those of the past; people still fight over land and resources, as they have for centuries.

Real-life travel has provided me with the opportunity to go beyond the textbook pages and actually *feel* history. As I climbed the time-molded steps of the Great Wall, I imagined a great siege taking place, Chinese soldiers in impossibly heavy armor running up and down the wall, warding off the Mongol invaders. I stood in awe at Westminster Abbey as I read the history of England in the engraved names of kings and queens buried there. In Salisbury Cathedral, a docent casually directed me to an original copy of the Magna Carta and was quite amused by my astonished and reverent reaction: "*the* Magna Carta?"

At seventeen years of age, I have just begun to explore the places I once only dreamed of. Each moment of wonder echoes the sense of promise and excitement I had as a child, picking up a brightly colored scarf and feeling the world at my fingertips.

COMMENTARY

Many college applicants face the challenge of tying together a myriad of extracurricular interests and academic pursuits in a single essay. This author chooses to explain with childhood dress-up games how she explores her "creative energy," crafting a consistent thread throughout the essay.

The author begins with a creative introduction with statements that clearly contradict one another: "I have traveled to many lands . . . while still eating home-cooked meals and sleeping in my own bed." Her conflicting claims leave the reader curious to know more. Details—from "a too-large checkered dress" to "turbans, shawls, and saris"—help paint a vivid image that ushers us into the author's world. The writer details the rich abundance of colors, fabrics, tastes, and visions she has had the privilege of partaking through dress-up, and these descriptions give the reader bites of the very imagination and creativity that the essay focuses on.

The author attempts to convey a single characteristic about herself—creativity—and makes content choices in line with this mission. Beginning with make-believe, transitioning to book reports as "artistic masterpieces," moving to theater, and ending with history, the writer draws a strong connection between the paths she has chosen to pursue.

The key to this essay lies at its end, when the author returns to her opening: "Each moment of wonder echoes the sense of promise and excitement I had as a child, picking up a brightly colored scarf and feeling the world at my fingertips." Here, she reminds readers that the path she has taken began with a single, imaginative moment. The author solidifies her essay as she closes the circle, creating a compelling and polished narrative arch.

—Molly M. Strauss

MARYKATE JASPER—"WHEN I WAS TEN"

When I was ten, my own grandma schooled me in Boggle. I had her beat by the time I was twelve. Boggle is a contest of vocabulary wherein the players wrest what words they can from sixteen given letters. I can still remember the word that bought my victory, W-R-E-N-S, a five-letter beauty worth two points. (All smaller words are only worth one point.)

Grandma had admittedly amassed an impressive hoard of four-letter words, peppered here and there with three-letter archaic jewels. Luckily, two summers of reading extensive historical fiction had readied my eye for spotting those antiquated gems, and I'd matched her word-for-word on that level. But she didn't find the game-winner W-R-E-N-S. After jotting down quickies like N-E-W and S-E-W, Grandma had forgotten to combine those letters, a fatal oversight. I beat her by one point.

This memory epitomizes my childhood: I was a fiercely competitive kid. Straight through middle school, my arch nemesis was Kevin, the blue-eyed math prodigy in the third row. Preaching male superiority with vehemence worthy of the pulpit, he would brag shamelessly about his grades. I was obsessed with outdoing him, not only for the sake of feminism, but for the sake of my pride. After all, I beat him soundly at reading comprehension, and his spellings were obscenely phonetic. What right had he to brag? I was the real genius.

Competition had long stewed in my blood by the time high school hit, and I had girded myself to vie with a new host of rivals. However, I was not prepared for the drama club, a troupe of girls who seemed shockingly indifferent to competition. At the first drama club meeting, no one seemed concerned about that afternoon's history test, though I recognized at least half of the freshmen from my class. Instead of chattering nervously about the answers, they were giggling belly-up on the auditorium floor or grinning atop the Steinway.

Didn't they care? Weren't they worried? I couldn't understand them, lounging indolently and teasing one another. And yet, I saw the fire of competition in them during auditions; it blazed in their gestures and ignited their high notes. But as they hopped off the stage, that bonfire shrank to a contented glow: I've done well. It was not an obsession for them, the quality of the performance versus the quality of other performances. It was done, closed and sealed; there was no use worrying whether their piece was the best. It was a personal best, and that seemed satisfaction enough.

Like stage makeup, they've rubbed off on me. Now I remember to lie belly-up, relaxed and content with my personal best instead of obsessing over whether I am #1. After all, B-E-S-T is only a four-letter word. One point.

COMMENTARY

This applicant's humorous take on a personality flaw manages to draw readers to her side as she demonstrates her personal growth. She could have benefited from tightening up the essay and drawing upon fewer anecdotes, but the essay still provides a colorful narrative that shows off the writer's creativity and maturity.

By opening with an anecdote about a competitive Boggle game against her grandmother, the applicant immediately sets an enjoyable, humorous tone for the essay. She also alludes to her own educational rigor, when she briefly mentions the two summers she spent reading "extensive historical fiction."

Throughout the next few paragraphs, the author describes the ups and downs of being competitive throughout her childhood. The light, self-deprecating tone of the writing keeps the reader on the applicant's side, even as she describes her fiercely competitive nature—a true feat.

But this essay could have benefited from the use of greater in-depth analysis of fewer anecdotes. Attempting to address even one anecdote with nuance and reflection in a short essay is difficult, and tackling three weakened this essay by leaving little room for detail of the applicant's conversion and growth.

Overall, the essay's humorous tone effectively complements its theme, and all the components for a successful essay are present. It only requires some tightening to present a more cohesive message. Still, the applicant manages to express maturity and growth—desirable qualities in any candidate.

—Frances Jin

Noah Hoch—"Bus Window Revelations"

Tree . . . tree . . . speed limit . . . tree . . . Exit 46 next left . . . tree . . . tree . . . light pole . . . tree . . .

That's pretty much how it goes on the bus rides to away games. I sit alone next to the window with my knees pressed up against the seat back in front of me. With one hand, I pick at the green duct tape that the bus driver used to cover the slice some delinquent cut into the strange material. With the other, I scroll through playlists on my iPod. Looking out the window, the trees just passing by, I can see the ghost of my face in the glass and I'm always reminded of those movies that begin with shots from inside a car, staring out at the fields of autumn trees, nature's memorial to the wilderness that once existed where the roads are now. As the credits fade in and fade out on the screen, always avoiding the direct center, a comfortable song like Peter Gabriel's "Solsbury Hill" just barely plays over the sound of tires on asphalt. For some reason, this is my favorite way for a movie to begin. I guess I like not knowing who the boy is in the car, but knowing that whoever he is, whatever he's doing, he's going somewhere.

I don't sit alone because I'm a recluse. Quite the contrary, I thrive when I'm around other people, and my best friends are all on the team. But, the bus has become the only place where I don't feel obligated to be working; it is a sanctuary for my thoughts, my imagination. In the passing fields my mind builds an entire metropolis and focuses in like a camera swooping down from a crane on a single boy, suitcase in hand, gawking at the intensity of a hundred-plus story steel mountain. It's his first time in the city and . . .

84

III. One Among Many: Presenting a Unique Applicant

Tree. The stick structure derails my train of thought and I am back on the bus. The interruption reminds me subtly that what I see through this transparent, glassed screen is only a figment. There is no reality out there in what I see . . . at least not yet.

On the bus, over the chatter of my teammates, my thoughts and my ideas may be fleeting and incomplete but they're enough to compel me to keep looking out the window. Someday, that's what I'll call my production studio: BUS WINDOW REVELATIONS. It will be a tribute to all those days where, past the water-splotched glass, I would see the two lovers finally reuniting, the once ambitious politician sitting at his desk crying tears of defeat, or the quiet resolve of an old man on his deathbed in the shadows of a mourning family. This is my imagination. This is my dream. This is who I am. I am reflected in the pane and I am reflected in movies behind it.

I like to think that I'm a lot like those movie beginnings. The credits roll like a silent "thank you" to all those who have put hard work into making me, but here the end of their work only becomes the beginning of my story. I'm that boy in the car. I don't know what he's doing, but I like that he's going somewhere. And for now, on the bus, I'm content to stare out the window, iPod in hand, and let the revelations come with each passing tree.

COMMENTARY

Harvard received over 29,000 applications for the class of 2013, and this essay is a great example of how to make your application stand out from the roughly 28,999 others. The author takes bits and pieces common to most applications—sports team, busy schedule, grand ambition—but imbues them with an introspective and personal glow that lights up what's behind his jam-packed résumé and stellar GPA.

We open on the image of the author looking pensive by the window of a school bus, but quickly move into the realm of metaphor and fantasy as the objects outside the window become a backdrop to the author's internal film screenings. The author treads lightly on the sports issue, giving us just enough for context but holding back so that it doesn't distract from what the essay is really about: his love of film. Through the rest of the essay, we move with the author back and forth between fantasy and reality. The writer affords us rare insight into his personality through the vehicle of his personal imaginations and fantasies—these are the types of creative outlets that define the writer, an individual who shows that he is inspired by the possibilities of film and the even more infinite range of his own potential.

At a few points, this essay gets bogged down with excessive detail. Descriptions like "the green duct tape that the bus driver used to cover the slice some delinquent cut into the strange material" give us a nice visual setting for the rest of the essay, but they tell us nothing about the author himself. At its best, his candid writing conveys the applicant's sincere dreams for the future: "I'm that boy in the car. I don't know what he's doing, but I like that he's going somewhere." All in all, this essay succeeds because it is a bus-window revelation of its own—of the boy behind the application.

—Jillian Goodman

Michael O'Leary—"Crossing the Rubicon? Child's Play"

The further back I look, the more my life reminds me of the opening of *The Wonder Years*—silent clips of WIFFLE ball in the driveway, wrestling with my brothers while Dad barbecues, even that girl with glasses and pigtails who trailed my every step. I'm pretty sure if I look back far enough I can even hear the faint murmur of Joe Cocker's chorus echoing in the background. But when I reminisce about endless summer afternoons and crustless peanut butter sandwiches, nothing shines more clearly than what happened one winter at West Elementary School. I was nine.

When I decided to run for president of the fourth-grade class, the die was not just cast, it'd already turned up a winner. I acted the politico part with promises, promises, and more promises. My bread and circuses would be chocolate milk at lunch, chalk at recess (to appease the four-square contingency), and enough dizzy-izzies at Field Day to get any kid sent home green. Having been caught too many times, I vowed that teachers would lose their right to read notes passed between secret admirers. I promised an end to the "No Eyes Closed" rule during reading time and, citing the 1934 Fair Labor Standards Act, I vowed to cut standardized test preparation by more than a third while more than doubling the length of the Halloween parade, the cultural high point of the fall term. "It's morning again in West School," I told them, and before I could even finish my first campaign speech the assembled electorate rose to its collective feet in a light show of stomping and flashing Velcro sneakers.

As voting day approached, I walked on proverbial air. I was becoming a real politician, a real huckster. I offered more hot cider than John Tyler offered hard. I was more common man than Jackson, more Camelot than Kennedy. I wrote better speeches on school buses than Lincoln on a train. When I'd walk the halls, third-grade girls would swoon and fifth-grade boys would nod in respect. Depending on with whom I spoke, I was left of FDR or right of Nixon all with a single word. I was the Father of the School, I was Uncle Mike, I was the Alpha and the Omega.

For years after, witnesses of the Great Schoolyard Debate of '99 recounted in hushed murmurs how I picked apart the deeply flawed economic assumptions in my opponents' "Free Balloon Day" campaign promise. They said I could win more votes with a single raise of an eyebrow than most could do with a Tupperware container of chocolate chip cookies.

"And congratulations to our new fourth-grade president, Michael O'Leary," the principal finally announced on the PA. My people had stayed true. I must've thanked all eighty-eight classmates that day twice-over. I held the will of the student body in the palm of my benevolent hand.

The shenanigans that had characterized the elementary school student council now came to an abrupt end. No longer were the convoluted cogs of democracy clogged with partisan politics. I bridged the boy/girl gap, the third-/fourth-grader gap, the Pokémon/Digimon gap. I even bridged the gap between the swing set and the water tower that had turned more ankles than Mrs. Mitchell's gym-class games of dodgeball. The finesse with which I managed the school's activity fund could've made Reaganomics look fiscally irresponsible. Under my reign, truancy hit all time lows. I both started and ended a War on Apathy. And indolence? Not on my watch.

But no sooner had I begun to usher in this dawn of a golden age than dark clouds formed on the horizon. Clashes among representatives broke out. Some called me a dictator. They called for restrictions on my powers—for my resignation! No heavy-handed clap of my gavel could hope to reestablish Robert's Rules of Order. I'm not sure if my rudder lacked a ship or their ship lacked my rudder, but my New Deal became No Deal. My Great Society became merely mediocre. The hot air of my campaign balloon had caught fire and turned disastrously reminiscent of the *Hindenburg*.

As the school year drained to an end, the very principal who'd announced my victory as president now told me that I would have to leave office when summer dawned. "Your turn is over," she said, as if my limited tenure had been fixed from the start! I felt it was a furtive move, yes, but someone had to play Brutus to my Julius Caesar. I had flown high, perhaps too high, as I now stood in a pile of melted wax and feathers, my literary allusions becoming more cliché by the minute.

Instead of rising up with an army of mudslinging preteens and reclaiming my "rightful" place, I recognized the rueful hand of Providence in my demise and stepped down, clutching at least my dignity and my honor.

Most of my peers recall nothing of my presidency a decade ago, nor do they recall the weeks-long tenure of the three fourth-grade presidents who preceded me or the four who followed. But I do, and that's what matters most. After all, history is written by its victors. And while the reality of my reign might be called into question, it stands apparent that my story is truer than true, that its so-called "reality" transcends mere facts or events. Tim O'Brien would be proud. Fade in Joe Cocker. Roll credits.

COMMENTARY

This essay stands out by portraying a relatively minor event that took place many years ago and would certainly not find its way onto a résumé, especially with its witty, satirical style. Chronicling the political process as it existed in elementary school, the writer frames his experiences using references from literature, politics, and television. His writing shows a sophisticated sense of humor.

By choosing a less-common topic and taking a lighthearted approach, the writer turns his childhood experience into a memorable story for his readers. The parallels the writer draws between fourth grade and real world politics—in terms of campaign promises, partisanship, glory, and finally, the fall to reality—demonstrate a unique perspective that many others with the same experience might not have captured. By frequently referencing political catchphrases, the writer is able to convey his interest in and knowledge of politics without directly saying so.

On the whole, this essay is quite compelling but could be improved by a few tweaks. Though the piece avoids the common mistake of attempting to deliver a moral in a heavy-handed way, it would have been strengthened by an explicit explanation for why this was such a noteworthy experience. As the essay stands, it does credit to the author in terms of the quality of the writing, but it is unclear why he chose to evoke memories of this subject in particular. Adding a few details about the meaningfulness of his experience would be helpful in this regard, while preserving the overall feel of the essay. However, these points do not detract from the quality of the writing or the personality of the writer, both apparent from reading the essay.

—Athena Jiang

EVAN ROSENMAN—"CREATIVITY, FAMILY, AND TOILET PAPER: A JOURNEY"

It stands about ten feet tall, towering over everything else in the front hall. It is covered in streaks of blue, tan, and white, and its ominous tentacles reach out in every direction. It is the stuff of an interior decorator's worst nightmare.

I refer, of course, to the sixteen-inch-diameter rope of entwined toilet paper that has been suspended from the second floor of my house for half a decade. Yes, you read that correctly. Toilet paper.

The creation of this veritable totem pole of hygienic glory began in seventh grade. On the day the project started, I was grounded. Frustrated at being forced to stay in the house, I unrolled a spool of toilet paper and hung it from the banister on the second floor. Soon, I had used up every roll in the house and had begun weaving them into a compact rope.

After that day, I periodically added to the rope until, eighteen months later, it had swelled to its current dimensions. The ever-expanding "sculpture"—as my mother called it, after she recovered from the initial shock—gradually became a fixture in our house. It no longer seemed out of place, juxtaposed against the polished banister, mauve carpet, and angular coat rack that surrounded it. Rather, it added character to the room, and, reciprocally, the room characterized it. Only when guests visited, gawking at the massive tree trunk of bathroom tissue, did we tend to notice its presence.

Yet, the rope is deeply significant to me. Its "fittingness," or comfortable position within more austere surroundings, has become an important symbol of my creativity, my identity, and my relationship with my family.

But let me start at the beginning. As the child of an attorney and an engineer-turned-patent attorney, I entered life with little creative guidance. My mother was drawn to math, my father to history, and my older brother to science, all from a young age. None were particularly inclined toward art, literature, or other imaginative pursuits.

I thus spent much of my early life immersed in my family's interests. I listened to my brother excitedly list "protons, neutrons, and . . . electrons!" at the dinner table; I paid close attention as my father explained the Battle of Trenton; and I happily did math problems in my head for my mother. I found myself intrigued by these subjects, but there was an oddity in the way I understood them. For instance, it perplexed my parents when I learned the word "tapestry" in grammar school and promptly declared, "Numbers are a tapestry!" My constant need to apply metaphors to science also suggested that I understood those subjects in a somewhat different context.

Then, as I grew older, I developed a strange sense that something was missing. It was an odd feeling, a sort of longing intermingled with random sounds and images rising meteorically in my mind and then fizzling away like a falling star. I could not identify this elusive interest for years, only sensing it as an unfulfilled desire, an unopened window. And then, suddenly, it came into focus when I began to study poetry. Within weeks of first encountering poetry in fifth grade, I devoured volumes of Shel Silverstein and moved on to more grown-up work: Denise Levertov, Billy Collins, Jane Cooper, and Walt Whitman would all become cherished influences. I also soon began to keep a ratty poetry journal, where I wrote wobbly but steadily improving stanzas each week.

The creative person I had discovered would most often wear the hat of a poet. Yet, he would also come to express himself through prose, filmmaking, and, on occasion, toilet-paper sculpting. And because I raised that creative person from infancy—my parents, while supportive, knew little about nurturing the imagination—my creative soul returned the favor by raising *me* up. Creativity became the outlet for my joy, frustration, and even my sadness.

But my creativity, much like the toilet-paper rope, was not untouched by its surroundings. Rather, it was characterized and defined by them. Thus, the interests my family had passed on to me became intricately tied to my creativity. After all, who could deny the poetic elements of an asymptote—that which is approached but never reached? Or the insight required to understand history, where trends must be extrapolated from mere events? These synergistic ideas became key to my understanding of the world, and for that, I have my family to thank.

The toilet-paper rope's lifespan is now approaching its end; I have an agreement with my parents that the fraying sculpture can finally be laid to rest once I depart for college. But I will always remember the rope for the part it played in the development of my unique identity. My family may have been befuddled by my strange creative streak (an accident of genetics, akin to my dirty-blond hair), but their influence and willingness to support me—even if that meant leaving a toilet-paper rope in the hall—has been a lasting gift.

COMMENTARY

Beginning an essay with a cold opener is a risky move, but this author pulls it off well by pulling it off quickly. The ambiguous, ominous "it" rewards the reader in the next paragraph with his description of a massive five-year-old toilet-paper structure. He builds his essay around this unusual object, using it as a jumping-off point to discuss his personal creativity, then tying it back in at the end. This is a creative and unpretentious way to tell admissions officers about a trait he possesses.

One weakness of this essay is its length—at over 830 words, it uses a lot of time and space to make its points. He spends five paragraphs setting up the introduction before starting "at the beginning." He then begins to describe each family member in detail to set up a mold that he will then shatter when he discovers poetry for the first time. However, that revelation comes too late for maximum effectiveness.

The real strength of this piece lies in its voice. The tone is natural and not at all contrived. The author's voice is authentic, much in the style of an old friend relating a personal story to the readers. For a college application essay, whose primary duty is to convey an accurate and appealing sense of the author's self, this essay excels at portraying an introspective, easily relatable young man, eager to explore his self through creative venues.

—Helen Yang

Jillian Goodman—"The Circle Game"

My butt is flattening on the cold linoleum floor, and I don't care. In fact, no one in the entire circle of fifty-six people cares an ounce that we've been sitting here for over an hour and a half. Most of us are seniors, and we want to suck every last moment from our final circle together.

The giant circle is a Retreat tradition. Every year on the first night of our three-day choreography weekend, we gather around a gigantic ball of rainbow-dyed yarn and every single person gets the chance to reveal what show choir means to him. The magic, though, is in the yarn. It starts out with a senior who says her piece and then throws the ball across the circle, holding on to the end. The next person makes his speech and then throws it again, keeping a loop around his finger. Then the next person speaks and throws the yarn, then the next, then the next—and soon boys are admitting they were intimidated by the beautiful sound and spectacular choreography of the Amazing Technicolor Show Choir, girls are crying over how show choir helped them find God or say good-bye to college-bound siblings, and a beautiful web has developed in the middle of the circle.

There are strands of all different lengths and color combinations, some lying uncomplicated on top of the web and some interlaced with innumerable others. You tug on your loop of yarn and you can see a person across the way respond. You lift your loop high and the rest of the group lifts with you. That's the way it is in our show choir. You ask for help and the person across the way responds. Something wonderful happens and the rest of the group shares it with you.

Looking at the web framing the linoleum reminds me of my very first show choir experience. An eight-year-old version of me sat on a floor very similar to this one and gaped at the middle-school show choir's two-part harmony and dazzling jazz squares. I still don't know what it was, but something inside me banged into life. For the rest of elementary school I knew that as soon as I made it to seventh grade I was going to be up there with my jazz hands and my thousand-watt smile, inspiring other eight-year-olds.

When the ball comes to me, I tell that story. And I tell everyone that in my sixth and final year on show choir I am just as excited as I was watching them nine years ago. Tears start to make the circle swim in my eyes because it would be impossible to relate the full depth of my feelings in any words that I know. As a freshman, I came into the school socially unsure and was immediately enveloped into this choir universe, and now as a senior crying over the memory, I am enveloped in an embrace.

I dry my eyes and pass on the yarn, clutching my very own piece of my very last web. When the last person has had his turn, our choir director comes around and snips every loop down the middle. We all hold on to the halves in our right hands, drop our lefts, and leave the circle with a part of the line that tied us all together for two hours on a Friday night into a Saturday morning. I use mine to reach back to the circle, to remind me that for an evening I wasn't the only one caring too much about something as fleeting as show choir. I use it to remember, because I don't get any more circles.

COMMENTARY

This essay is well written and exemplifies one of the most important qualities that admissions officers look for in applicants: convincing passion. Students should be wary of writing about topics

III. One Among Many: Presenting a Unique Applicant

they are not truly passionate about, as it is easy to spot insincerity in cases like, "I went to a foreign country for a week on a school trip and discovered an unbridled passion for global health." But in this case, the writer clearly loves show choir, and it shines through in her piece.

The author's story about the giant circle showcases the impact show choir has had on her life. She demonstrates her lifelong devotion to show choir when she describes how "something inside [her] banged to life" when she first experienced it as an eight-year-old. This isn't just a story she is telling to impress the admissions officers, but one she has also shared with the other members of her show choir. The writer's emotions are genuine, and they show the reader how passionately devoted she can be to an activity she loves.

While her conclusion—in which she writes that she saved the yarn because "she does not get any more circles"—conveys the depth of her feelings for show choir, it makes the essay end on a sad and confusing note. A more optimistic ending about looking forward to putting her heart into other endeavors and deriving the same sort of life-altering experience from future pursuits would seem more appropriate, but if this is not the case, then it is always better to be honest and candid. While a disingenuous essay may slip by the admissions officer, it is not a risk worth taking.

—Ravi Mulani

Steven Roach—"Concerto in C Minor"

I am a piano player of three years, but a composer of my life. Amassing numerous piano awards and receiving applause after a performance cannot equal the time spent composing the masterpiece of life. "Dedicated," "driven," "determined" are words that some would use to describe me, but never "uncertain." Uncertain of how I will play in front of an audience. Uncertain that I will ever live up to the expectations that others set for me. But most of all, uncertain of where my life will lead me.

As my fingers glide up the C major scale while playing the piano, I realize that my fingers remain on the white keys and never give the black keys a chance to voice their tune. I try to add one of the black keys to the scale, and cringe at the dissonant, frightful, yet intriguing sound it causes. Despite my initial reaction, I still cannot fully understand why the major keys get to be played while the minor keys are relegated to the background, hidden between and behind the white keys. I want to know why the white keys get all of the attention. I want to know the reason for assigning the white keys as major keys. I want to play the black keys.

I have green eyes, and my skin is whiter than that of some Caucasian people, but I still cannot forget my African-American roots. One of my grandmothers is white, but both of my parents are black. Even when the tension of being black gets as tight as one of the taut wires in the piano, I cannot forget the minor parts of my keyboard, no matter how conflicting they may be with the white keys. Even though my skin may resemble that of a white person, my phenotype remembers its genotype when I play the piano: The major part of me is black while the minor part of me is white.

Throughout my life, the blend in my genes has reflected the blends of culture in my life. Growing up in Willingboro, New Jersey, a predominantly black neighborhood, I embraced the black parts of me. From the history of segregation that the neighbors' stories depicted to my own memories of the kids playing basketball on the courts, I came to experience a part of my culture. Thrown into a discordant community at my Episcopal school in a mainly white neighborhood, I learned about the other side of me, the side that everyone could see, but that I could not feel. The blend in my school and home life has composed the best song, a song that needs those black keys to form the right tune.

The best musical pieces, as any pianist can attest, mix a combination of the black and white keys to produce harmonic tones. American society, and humanity in general, cannot play one part of itself while ignoring the other key parts. The black keys do not produce sounds of fright and dissonance whenever played, but a sonorous sound of richness, emotion, and complexity. Without each complement, both black and white keys would be left separated, never being able to harmonize and produce the best tune for the world to hear.

Wherever life takes me, I'm ready. I am dedicated, driven, determined, and even uncertain. My spirit no longer feels the weight of the piano's tiny hammers knocking as they vibrate the wires of the inner piano. Just like the best composers, I continue to push forward, not knowing what lies ahead, but understanding that if I keep writing the piece, it will end on the right note.

COMMENTARY

In this essay, the writer suggests that the black and white keys of a piano provide insight into his own mixed heritage. At first, the analogy creates an intriguing parallel between the writer's fervor for music composition and his desire to reclaim his sometimes eclipsed African-American heritage. "[M]inor keys are relegated to the background, hidden between and behind the white keys," just as his African-American heritage is pushed aside both in his physical appearance and in his parochial school. The analogy remains compelling up to this point. But it should have ended there.

This applicant has a fascinating story to tell. He is three-quarters African-American but can easily be mistaken for white. He attended school in a white neighborhood but lived in an African-American one, adding an extra dimension to his mixed upbringing. But the author only touches on these subjects, mentioning them in the context of his passion for the piano. His upbringing is itself sufficiently compelling to stand without the crutch of the piano metaphor. Throwing in some telling anecdotes about instances when he questioned or struggled with his racial identity would have propelled this essay from solid to outstanding.

A point of weakness is the analogy itself that the writer relies upon heavily. The comparison has initial utility but ultimately stymies some of the excellent writing and imagery in this piece. By confining the piano analogy and establishing his passion for the instrument in the beginning paragraphs, he would have left himself space later in the essay to delve deeper and explore the many facets of the internal conflict he faced in his youth. In short, the old standby of "less is more" rings especially true in this case, particularly when one is working with metaphors. The author could

III. One Among Many: Presenting a Unique Applicant

have drawn far more capital from his experiences by moving beyond the limitations of the metaphor and making room for greater self-exploration.

—Laura Mirviss

Andrew Pacis Wong Gonzales— "Ziggurat"

On my desk are four books stacked in order of size. My Chinese-English dictionary, with its striking vermillion cover, grabs my attention. Its pages, filled with flowing Chinese characters and rigid English print, remind me of the two cultures that shape me—East and West. I am a Chinese, Filipino Texan. On family picnics, I enjoy cheeseburgers while stuffing my face with moon cakes and *lumpia*, Filipino egg rolls. I use both chopsticks and a knife when eating steak. I am *that* student who will jump into college with one arm wrapped around a toaster and the other lugging a rice cooker by its electrical cord. I tap my feet to Chinese and Japanese pop, as well as strut my viola to classical Mendelssohn tunes. In the spring, I row in my school's crew team and participate in dragon boat races. For New Year, I greet my parents: *"kong shi fa chai,"* expecting to receive a red Chinese envelope filled with green American dollars. My eastern and western backgrounds are like yin and yang, pushing and pulling, weaving the harmonious whole that is me. I am a *halo-halo*, a Filipino word that means mixture within a mixture.

Underneath my dictionary lies *Physics of the Impossible*. Its pages peer into the distant future of invisibility cloaks and quantum computers. This book expresses why I love science: its ability to improve the future. My surroundings, from the infinite cosmos to the invisible atoms that compose it, derive their elegance from scientific laws. My body is a mammoth Petri dish, a conglomerate of specialized cells, bubbling with energetic reactions. Since I cannot escape science, I fully embrace it by my obsession in nanotechnology. I first delved into this world while conducting research at the Welch

III. One Among Many: Presenting a Unique Applicant

Summer Scholars Program. I was struck by the unbelievably precise control I had over the environment. I manipulated organized layers of nanoparticles, changing their properties at will. With the click of a mouse, I took "atomic snapshots" of my samples, allowing me to study arrangements of molecular clusters. I believe nanotechnology will be the wave of the future, and one day, I hope to be at its forefront, surfing that wave. I envision creating computer programmed "nanobots" that can repair damaged heart and nerve tissues. I could engineer a noninvasive surgery by strategically placing "nanochips" in the body that would single out and destroy cancer cells once detected. The possibilities appear endless as I pull out my book and scribble my dreams onto its margins.

At the bottom, my hefty study Bible supports the entire stack. It mirrors my sturdy moral foundation. My precious pocket Bible sits at the top of the stack. I always carry it, as I do my values. Together, the Bibles sandwich the other books in the pile. They demonstrate how my principles keep my passions in check, enabling me to walk discerningly through life, while simultaneously seeking truth and knowledge. The desire to serve motivates me to be involved in community service, to aid the homeless and the disabled. It is compassion that empowers me to rise every Saturday morning to volunteer at a pediatric hospital in Dallas. Charity compels me to save my allowance in order to donate several hundred dollars to earthquake victims in Szechuan, China. With integrity, I serve as chairman of my school's Discipline Council, charged with the task of upholding the school's honor code, recommending penalties to those who violate it. The awareness that I am imperfect and that life is fleeting keeps me humble. No matter how life changes, my values remain the same. They give me the motivation to improve myself and others.

My books tower like a miniature ziggurat, each work adding a distinct step to the terraced temple's overall structure. Similar to my books, my passions, insights, and ideals form the individual building blocks that establish my identity. In many ways, I am akin to a library, filled with nonfiction stories and distinctive accounts that vary in drama and suspense. Over the course of a lifetime, I write my own unique plots through my daily actions. Each moment is a romance, mystery, or adventure waiting to be read. So next time someone says he can read me like a book, I will vigorously pump his hand and say, "Pleased to meet you."

COMMENTARY

This essay earns points for framing the applicant through original means. By seizing on treasured books to narrate, the applicant gives the reader a real sense of his passions, heritage, and aspirations. The series of examples he gives, particularly at the beginning, carry a real momentum that propels the reader through the essay. In a pile of applications, admissions officers will see dozens upon dozens of essays touting multicultural identities. It's crucially important to stand out. This essay accomplishes that aim by putting forward a thought-provoking metaphor for the applicant. Remember always that readers spend minutes, not hours on your writing. Be interesting.

Another particularly compelling portion of the essay is the treatment of spirituality embodied by the two Bibles the writer owns. He explains how his Christian morals and principles allow him to navigate through life's challenges and give him a sense of purpose. Overall, the multiple layers of the author's identity shine through in the essay and make the applicant seem alive and approachable.

Though the applicant obviously won the admissions officers in the end, it is worth noting that the essay suffers from grammatical errors ("my obsession *in* nanotechnology"). Certainly, such flaws are not enough to completely discredit an otherwise compelling essay, but applicants should take the time to carefully proofread their pieces before submission to make sure that small mistakes do not aggregate into a larger problem with the writing. It is worth your time to check for grammatical consistency in a piece that can tip the scale on where you spend the next four years of your life.

Briefly, this essay serves as a great introduction to the writer. It deals with sensitive topics such as race and religion, but in the end gives the reader a great sense of who the applicant is, where he comes from, and where he intends to be in the future. The writer's anecdotal examples make his voice better heard in the essay, and he uses this voice to display his talent, potential, and originality. Overall, the essay describes what is most important to and about the applicant, which makes it an effective component of a college application.

—Elias Shaaya

MOLLY KELLY—"TODDLER COUTURE"

With endless colors to choose from, a glamorous, sparkly shine, and the unparalleled ability to create spectacular scuff marks on your mom's prized wooden floors, a staple in any fashionable young girl's wardrobe is the patent leather shoe. This shoe, often overlooked and almost never fully appreciated, is the go-to solution for all moms in need—it goes with *any* party dress, and their daughters always adore the selection! When I was a young girl, my style was no exception to this continuing trend—I wore these shoes with many an outfit. However, my childhood fashion experiences were rather heightened by something not so typical: my intense, border-line aberrant obsession.

I can't remember the exact details of the day that started it all, but I do have a hazy recollection. On those weekend days that you devote entirely to errands, my mom always dragged my cranky five-year-old self with her to each store written on her to-do list. On the day in question, there was an unexpected stop: the shopping mall. In the Stride-Rite shoe store, our destination, there is no doubt in my mind that I scowled and whined belligerently at having to place my foot on the cold metal measure to find my size. However, my mom obviously forced me through it, and we left the store with my new black shoes, wrapped in confetti tissue paper and nestled in a green shoebox.

At home, with these wondrous, magical shoes ensconcing my small feet, my infatuation bloomed. I don't know what it was— maybe the unique luster or perhaps their dainty flowery cutouts?— but something about them captivated my attention. No matter what

III. One Among Many: Presenting a Unique Applicant

the occasion, I wore them with an effervescent, immutable glow and flaunted them incessantly. Quite simply, I thought my "party shoes" were the coolest!

When bedtime arrived, I refused to take the shoes off. "They're too pretty!" I would stubbornly resist. All of my mother's efforts to convince me otherwise were futile. So, she acquiesced, and I, reveling in my glorious success, wore them with my Barbie nightgown and hopped between my pink sheets with a contented smile. However, after I fell asleep, my mom would always sneak back into my room, pry the shoes from my feet, and place them back in the closet where they belonged.

When my mom took my shoes from me, I was *not* happy. In the throes of my indignant angst, I thought it was the deepest form of betrayal. But, the driven never accept defeat. If my mom took my beloved shoes from me, I would spring from my bed and scour the room, searching passionately until I found them. Inevitably, by the following morning, I would be wearing my shoes once more.

Today, I am happy to say that I am no longer addicted to wearing shiny black party shoes. And, I can confidently tell you that my passions and desires are far less materialistic and selfish. However, my determination has not wavered; to this day, it is this single trait that carries me forward. My drive, previously centered on my adorable patent leather shoes, has intensified and redirected itself to cover a wide range of activities—whether it's my tennis serve, Spanish-speaking skills, or political acumen, if I am ever dissatisfied with something, I devote myself completely to perfecting it.

In the future, I doubt I'll be furiously pushing for a reunion with a pair of shoes. Patent leather just isn't my style anymore! However, rest assured: With whatever path I choose, I will do everything within my power to succeed. And, just as important, I will be wearing some *killer* stilettos.

COMMENTARY

The author's well-thought-out piece accomplishes with ease what any college essay should first and foremost aim to do: display the author's ability to write clearly and effectively. She displays her facility with language, imbuing her essay with colorful details and quirky observations, like the all-important patent leather shoes and her mother's "prized wooden floors." The writer describes this peculiar pastime with a familiar and comfortable ease, inviting the reader into her world. In discussing her affinity for fashion as a young girl, the writer goes one step beyond simple storytelling and clues the admissions officers in to one aspect of her personality through a fun and fanciful recollection.

The essay's greatest strength lies in its author's descriptive abilities, coupled with her charm and humor. Whether she is reminiscing about a shoe-shopping adventure with her mother or recounting the physical details of her patent leather sandals, the author carries the reader to the scenes of her youth with a mature and well-developed voice, balanced with a childlike fancifulness that ensures that the essay does not fall too deep into the common mold of the serious college essay. Through her careful usage of both adult language and controlled humor, the author is able to convey a convincing whimsy that few others would be able to generate.

Furthermore, her attention to detail—sentences such as "I . . . wore them with my Barbie nightgown and hopped between my pink sheets with a contented smile"—ensures that the admissions officers are left with a clear picture of her girly and happy-go-lucky nature. But it's not merely her use of description—the author is selective about her details, careful to choose images that most accurately depict her character.

However, the essay ultimately reverts to referencing overused clichés in its concluding paragraphs. The writer relies on stating outright to the reader that she is a determined and persistent person. This issue may stem from her need to establish a more direct link between her determination to wear her patent leather shoes and her drive to succeed in other aspects of her life, perhaps suggesting that her topic choice may have been a weak metaphor for displaying this aspect of her character. Indeed, the downfall of a topic choice that makes itself an optimal subject of humor is the potential problem of an essay that strives too hard to connect the humor with the profound, the whimsy with the meaningful. Despite this concern, this piece ultimately succeeds in showcasing her writing abilities and her humorous and fun-loving personality.

—Lucy Chen

ALEX KIM—"STILL LIFE"

Barely sloshing, my jars shudder into the light. The technician turns the crank once more. Space is precious here, so these shelves are collapsible. At rest, they bunch up like the wrinkles in my pulled-up sleeves—tense, expectant. Waiting for someone like me, who'll edge in between them, lean in to scan a yellowed museum label, then step back to take it in all at once: the sealed glass containers, the amber-stained alcohol and the ghostly crustaceans within. These jars are cool to my touch, and the room is fireproofed against their contents.

My electronic card key says VISITING SCIENTIST, SMITHSONIAN INSTITUTION. I had smiled at how smoothly the padlocked doors clicked open, but now the key is oddly heavy in my pocket. Through my backpack, familiar rectangular lumps nestle against my spine. The boxy case of my electronic calipers. Jeweler's tweezers and a scalpel in a zippered leather pouch. A digital camera, forever set to macro (to capture tiny bristles and spines). My notebooks, muddy and misshapen from run-ins with river water.

I set the first jar on my worktable.

As I twist open a lid sealed decades before my birth (it feels like desecration), I hear a doubtful voice, mostly my mother's—but my own as well. *Shrimp?* (The very word, I know, smacks of insignificance.) What's more to *shrimp* than dead shellfish, headless and gray on a briny slab of supermarket ice? Isn't science supposed to be cancer and computer simulations? Why limit yourself—why not study something *big*?

Yes, I always was drawn to the "small things," the creatures you'd never see on a World Wildlife Fund poster—that you'd have to get down on hands and knees to see at all. On my first visit to the zoo, elephants and giraffes barely registered; I plowed through that throng of knees straight to the insect house. Aged five, in the tall grass behind our house, I filled dozens of jam jars with the *plink* of tiny jointed claws. I think back to those early weekly trips to the library, of clutching books with titles like *Spineless Wonders* and *Insect Masquerades*. I pause.

Gingerly, I lift him from the jar of preservative. The years have wearied him, turned him brittle. With index finger and thumb, I tug the stirring sleeper into air that knew him last half a continent and a century before.

Shrimp belittles him. He is a spiny beast tipped at one end with a saw-toothed prow and at the other with a fluked tail like the petals of an ivory rose. From between his stalked eyes sprouts a spindly bouquet of antennae. His fingers curve like thorn-studded hooks and his bleached flesh is the color of apricots. The mortician's tag is a soggy rectangle of parchment. With my jeweler's forceps, I flip it to read the spidery cursive on its other face. SANTA MARIA, VERACRUZ, MEXICO. FEBRUARY 14, 1894. The ink has barely run.

I am here to reduce him to measurements of limbs and trunk, to a data point. But as I angle my calipers over his shell, I see him as he was in life, cream-colored stripes streaking his sides and China orange in all his many joints. I see him in his infancy, a speck of plankton flushed with a million siblings from the headwaters of his birth to the palm-fringed lagoon of his childhood. I see him make the long slog upstream, scrabbling up cascades and over riverbanks, learning to shelter from herons and stick-wielding boys in undercut banks and catfish tunnels. I see him raising his outspread claws as the naturalist's dip-net looms overhead. I see him at the moment of death, thrown unceremoniously into a tub of formalin. He flexes like a harpooned whale, splashing his collector's cotton shirt, and then is quiet. The color's still fresh in his shell.

Measurements finished, I snap shut the stainless-steel jaws of my calipers. The spines and fluted ridges of the creature on my tray, this time traveler from bygone waters, murmur softly to my eyes. Limiting myself? I shake my head. In these swimmerets, there is poetry.

COMMENTARY

Applicants often make the assumption that the best college essays showcase an individual's personal strengths and successes in a highly transparent and shamelessly triumphant manner, not realizing that people can often reveal their true and most vibrant colors by taking a more oblique approach in writing about themselves. This is the method employed by this applicant, and to great effect. The entire piece revolves around the simple act of examining a preserved shrimp from the late 1800s: surely one of the dullest—not to mention, literally lifeless—topics one can choose to expound upon. However, the writer capitalizes upon the irony of the situation, as evinced by the clever title, "Still Life," to suggest that vivacity exists beneath that spiny and crusty exterior, and that life reverberates in unexpected places. Through his exposition about the ancient crustacean, he adeptly convinces readers that he possesses the rare insight that allows him to perceive life in places where few others would see it. His essay may be about a shrimp, but it is actually a meditation on his unique ability to revivify the dead and unstudied through his sincere passion for the sciences. The writer does not simply inform the reader of his academic interests; rather, he conveys the very impact of such passions on his vision of the world around him.

He writes, "In these swimmerets, there is poetry"—and his language deftly proves as much. That said, there is always a risk in beginning an essay too obliquely and leaving the reader confused and disoriented, which the writer does, but he manages it by quickly providing a setting and context for his scene in the very next paragraph. The applicant does not simply describe for the sake of showing how well he can write; he uses his language with the pointed motivation of displaying, through words, the life he sees in the preserved shrimp. His descriptive language is effective not merely for its richness and creativity, but for its ability to evoke his feelings.

An especially strong passage is when he describes the shrimp as he sees it. Its creepy antennae "sprout" like a "bouquet," and its tail flukes are like an "ivory rose." The writer indeed brings poetry to the most unexpected of items. His essay invites readers to share his vision of the shrimp and to understand how he sees life, and through the uniqueness of this perspective, this applicant persuades readers that he possesses a vision that few other applicants can boast of.

—Esther Yi

Joe Sullivan—"Untitled"

"Why," he asked, "did you find Cambodia so interesting?" After a satisfying in-flight meal, I had begun chatting with the stranger seated to my right. Despite my kindergarten teacher's warnings, I talk to strangers whenever I can—eighteen years of living have convinced me that chance encounters are simply too important to do otherwise. This Belgian salesman returning from business in Bangkok was no exception.

I had developed a repertoire of simple answers to his question: the intriguing modern history, the fascinating Khmer culture, the off-the-beaten-path-ness. None were lies and all were convenient, but none were the whole truth. I liked this guy and I had time, so I gave him a full answer. To fully understand my answer to his question, first accompany me for a quick stroll into the past.

It's safe to say that as a young boy I visited a speech therapist more often than most. I used to speak at a dazzlingly high and unintelligible rate, churning out words faster than most people type. If I slowed down, I stuttered. These childhood speech delays are no longer audible in the way I speak, and I have since outgrown them. But their legacy persists, affecting how I think about language and its relationship with the world.

Ten years ago, a thought would wade into my stream of consciousness, splashing around for a while before wanting to move on. The feisty thought would then itch and poke at my mind, gnawing away as it begged to be put into words and shared with the world. Having a speech disorder made that last part painfully difficult at times. Whereas most children simply spoke whatever words rolled through their head, I found myself searching for the words I thought would be easiest for me to say—I had more trouble on certain sounds—if I decided it was worth the effort at all.

Because the process of attaching words to thoughts was a drawn-out and conscious process for me, at a young and impressionable age I realized that language is as separable from what it describes as the number six is from six apples or a Monet painting is from a lily pond. Words, I realized, were simply fluid and convenient tools of description. This enabled me to develop an appreciation for the artistic potential of the written word, to see beyond its rigid, pragmatic, mundane face and into its creative, ambiguous, abstract soul. Just as a painter like Dalí exploits his physical dexterity to pour his imagination onto the canvas, so did I exploit the linguistic dexterity I acquired as a result of my speech issues, as I let my young imagination bleed ink-black onto the white page. At this point, my speech difficulties became a gift, providing lifetime benefits for me as a writer as I enjoy a heightened sensitivity to the nuances of language.

While I appreciate the artistic value of language, I have also grown to believe there is something invariably lost when, in that precious instant, the human mind attaches word to thought. Art provides subjective beauty, not objective fact, and translation always has its victims. This realization had interesting ramifications for my study of history and anthropology, longtime interests of mine. When I read a scholar's discussion of Chinese attitudes toward government, for example, I could not help but wonder if the seven-letter word "respect" wraps fully around this complex and ancient issue. In time, I developed a nagging desire to travel to the places I studied, to feel the stares of their people and to walk down their streets instead of reading somebody else's words about them. And, in my opinion, no other nation could match the exciting blend of social forces and historical realities swirling around in Cambodia this past July. I couldn't resist.

So, why did I find that sweltering, impoverished corner of Southeast Asia called Cambodia so interesting? Because for so long I had wanted to experience such an intriguing nation for myself. To feel the heartbeat of a fledging and rowdy young democracy during the national elections it held during my stay, and not just read a UN election observer's report. To hear the wind whisper of the Khmer Rouge as I walked through the killing fields, not read about the ineffable atrocity. To see the wonder in the weathered eyes of its people as I showed them images from my distant home, not read generalizations about their personalities. To see the shadows of Angkor Wat dance with the ghosts of Pol Pot in a land where, in a bizarre paradox, ancient majesty and modern poverty peacefully coexist, not read dry economic statistics.

The Belgian man simply nodded. I hope he understood my English.

COMMENTARY

If not a paradox, it's at least a curiosity: a dense, language-rich piece about the limits of language itself. As far as college essays go, this one waxes fairly philosophical. "Words, I realized, were simply fluid and convenient tools of description," the author writes; one gets the sense that he would really enjoy the linguistic anthropology classes on offer here.

It's easy to imagine such ruminations growing heavy. But the essay's exemplary structure helps it all hang together—the author provides a solid backbone to his more intangible perspectives on language. An essay that simply dives into one's love for language runs the risk of falling into indecipherable vagueness, but this writer couches his passion for language within the interaction with the man and his interest in Cambodia, giving flesh to what could have been an otherwise hard-to-describe passion. Furthermore, a narrative about the writer's reasons for traveling to Cambodia lightens the intensity of the prose and gives the meditations on language a place to hang their hat. An anecdote about striking up a conversation with a stranger on the flight home draws the reader in from the start and serves as a brilliant launching pad for the reflections on his childhood that follow. And the last line—if a tad flip—succeeds in looping back to the introduction to provide a neat bit of symmetry.

Crucially, the lyrical effusions always find consistent backing in concrete example. Of all the suggestions that can be made to college essay writers staring down a blank page, the most useful is probably this: include as much colorful detail as possible. Imagine an admissions officer in his swivel chair on Brattle Street (or whatever the equivalent is at University X). It's been a long day of wading through transcripts and trying to determine whether the zillionth community-service club presidency entails any duty more involved than writing one's name on an extracurricular sheet. In short, he's exhausted, and there are still two hours to go before it's time to punch out. The last thing he wants is a dull metaphysical exegesis to cross his desk at the eleventh hour.

This essay could've been too much—too verbose, too broad-ranging, too poetic. But its concreteness keeps its flights of fancy grounded enough, and the enthusiasm with which its ideas are expressed helps it stay believable. Ultimately, it can be checked off as a definitive success: complex, yet clear enough to engage any reader, real or imagined.

—Jessica Sequeira

ROBERT THWAITS—"COLLEGE ESSAY"

A senior's worst fear: the dreaded college essay. You can even call it
the bane of my existence. But that's too dramatic. And dramatic is
bad, or so I'm told. Yet, the significance of these five hundred words
cannot be denied. As one admissions officer kindly informed me,
"Your essay can make or break your application for you. Write it
wisely." No pressure.

I panicked. I dreamed of sitting down in front of my laptop on
some sunny, bright afternoon, clacking out an essay on the keyboard.
After all, the college essay is just a sample of my writing, right? Instead, I frantically ran around asking for advice from friends and family, sort of like a startled rat in a maze, but not nearly as furry.

"Write about a once-in-a-lifetime experience. Describe how you
came from China just before turning nine, knowing nothing but the
alphabet, and proceeded to conquer the English language," my mom
suggested. "Be sure to include how this difficult obstacle has shaped
you and given you determination and confidence to succeed in your
endeavors," she added.

"Colleges like continuity. Show the college your passion for Chinese culture and music through your eight years of playing the
Chinese hammered dulcimer," said a friend over ice cream. "You are
second chair in your orchestra, aren't you?"

Upon hearing this conflicting advice, I sank deeper into the
ubiquity of a dark, engulfing abyss. Scratch that—too dramatic. But
I was definitely confused. As a solution to my problem, I finally
settled on a mini anthology of successful application essays that I
had picked up in the local bookstore. To my dismay, however, the

opening words of the book were, "There is no one foolproof method for writing a winning admissions essay." As a matter of fact, "most of the advice you are given will contradict itself." Great. Back to square one.

So over the next week (so much for a short sunny afternoon), I scrutinized the book, one great essay at a time. There were ones narrating vivid memories of remarkable events, and there were ones depicting personal tragedy handled with such strength and maturity. Of course, each piece was unique in its own way. Finding some common thread linking those literary jewels together was impossible, though I can't say I didn't try.

My plan for the perfect essay went down the drain. It was back to the drawing board, as the cliché goes. Thus beaten before I even began, I started trying to capture my personality in roughly five hundred words. I wrote several essays, each covering some facet of who I am. Yet none screamed out to me, "I'm the right essay, pick me!" Much as cells varied in function come together to produce that emergent property we call life, so my essays together formed a synergy greater than the sum of its parts—me. It was then that I had an epiphany of sorts. The college essay isn't an autobiography describing who I am; it is about being who I am.

Now that I look at the college essay as something along the lines of a personal ad, it's not nearly as daunting. Here is who I am: I'm five feet nine inches, with jet-black hair and deep mahogany eyes. I enjoy soccer, economics, and long walks on the beach gazing at a romantic sunset. . . . Oops, wrong type of personal ad.

COMMENTARY

Fans of '90s sitcoms will remember the episode of *Seinfeld* where Jerry and George are sitting in an NBC office struggling to cast actors for their new show peculiarly fashioned after *Seinfeld* itself as a show about nothing. Well, the gimmick worked, and the episode was a success.

Breaking the fourth wall, whether in television or in writing, is risky, but this author pulls it off by writing an essay about writing his essay. Not only that, but he does it humorously and intelligently in a manner that also conveys multiple aspects of his personality, his heritage, and his interests.

We learn much about the writer. An immigrant from China, he was at a disadvantage compared to his peers when it came to reading. He quickly caught on but held on to his Chinese roots, playing an instrument unheard of in the United States but native to his homeland. He doesn't tell us this directly, which makes this compelling story all the more honest and all the less boastful. Moreover, his intellect shines from his seemingly casual mentioning of cell biology, economics, music, and appreciation for "literary jewels."

Underlying this essay's success is the ease with which it can be read. The variety of forms of delivery—dialogue, narrative, and a smattering of after-thoughts—does not leave readers bored, and the humor makes the essay enjoyable. The ideas in each successive sentence are fresh, and with a pace that's quick, a tone that's light, and a topic that's fun, the character of a high school senior who's well rounded, talented, humble, witty, personable, and ultimately a likely-to-be positive contributor to Harvard's campus surfaces.

But maybe that's too dramatic—and dramatic is bad, so we're told.

—Naveen Srivatsa

CHRISTIAN FLOW—"HEADLINES, HERODOTUS . . . AND FULL-FIELD SPRINTS"

June 2005

Imagine walking into a house and being handed five or six texts, each as thick as a balled-up fist: the next six weeks of your life, in print and paper binding. Herodotus, Thucydides, Aeschylus, Aristophanes. For me and fifteen other students from around the country, these were to be the primary professors, the foundation upon which we would build our thoughts and our days. There were no air-conditioning units, no televisions, no pools or parties or pinups of teen-idols, or any of the other trappings of a residential summer camp. But in their place there were the texts, the notebooks, and each other.

It was the "each other" that may have been the most difficult part of the experience. My fellow "TASPers" were not like my friends at home, many of whom scoffed at my choice of plans before heading off to their beach houses and summer jobs and lacrosse camps. And in a way this was refreshing. But I soon became frustrated with the notion that I was constantly subject to the group's approval. When I wanted to go to a student-center across campus to watch the MLB All-Star Game, the idea had first to be debated in a house-meeting. When I wanted to use a small amount of community money to purchase a set of weights for the house, a similar procedure ensued. On one occasion, my mother wanted to come visit me for a couple of hours, and even that had to be duly reported and discussed. Still, these are the struggles of existing in a community, the sort of trials upon which progress as a person is necessarily based. And though we sometimes clashed and disagreed, I wouldn't have had it any other way.

Late August 2005

Eight o'clock in the morning and I was panting, my shirt already a sweaty mess, my heels host to a horde of blisters, as I labored end-line-to-end-line-and-back (some 240 yards) across a turf field that shimmered in the morning heat. Eleven times we did this: once for each of the league wins the coach was hoping to record. And that was just to cap off a morning practice: 12:45 and I'd be back out here again. Summer soccer workouts have a way of becoming an all-day affair.

This is what all my daily runs and pushups in the driveway and sit-ups on the rug amount to—an opportunity to get on the field and practice with the team. It isn't about playing time or scoring goals, because in fact I've never been able to crack the starting lineup. But it is very much an occasion to push myself to the limit. To the coach, it looks like just another sprint, but to me the burning sensation, the soreness is a signal that I'm doing something right, that I've taken control of my life and am living out my moments the way I deem most fitting: end-line-to-end-line, limited rest in between.

September 2005

Soccer practice was over for the evening. I stretched, showered, changed, and walked across campus toward the Upper School building. I was tired. The day had begun at three in the morning with a particularly long reading that I had been unable to address before drifting off the night before. Now there was more homework to be done, but first the school newspaper had to be finalized. I was comforted by the knowledge that once I began working, moving the words around on the screen to iron out those last little flaws, all the fatigue would disappear.

There's simply no time to be tired when you're doing the things you love, especially when it's impossible ever to feel established in any of those pursuits. I firmly believe that if ambition is to be edifying, it must center on the inherent and humbling realization that it will always fail to reach its end. I have tried to fill my days as a student, tried to live life like a full-field sprint. But in the end, there are always more sprints that could have been run, more wise words that could have been read, more stories that could have been reported. And what of my interactions with others? Can ambition not be brought to bear here as well? Could I not reach ceaselessly to be a better member of a community like TASP, a better teammate, a better editor to the newspaper staff? It is these sorts of questions that drive me, making the long days seem so short. And it is the motivation they create that I plan to carry with me as I continue my education.

COMMENTARY

It's one thing to overcome a challenge, but it's quite another to embrace it, to take advantage of it in a way that makes it an experience you desire more of. In this essay, the writer displays a peculiar knack for studying at odd hours, running until blisters appear on his feet, and tiring himself to the point of fatigue. With a simple, yet unique, chronological organization, the writer takes the reader through several snapshots of his life, all moments that capture his intensity, drive, and focus. But this is not merely an essay about how hard he works, or a declaration of his devotion to his studies and athletics.

The crux of the essay pivots upon the writer's acknowledgment of his own insufficiencies. He does not rest comfortably upon the laurels of his work and his achievements, whether on the field or on the school newspaper, to trumpet the depth of his dedication; rather, he uses his vivid experiences of pouring sweat and sheer exhaustion as platforms upon which he cannot and will not rest. The already established intensity of the writer's character makes his desire to exceed himself all the more notable—and all the more remarkable. This is not a retrospective essay that seeks to boast of accomplishments and past records; instead, this is an essay that forges a way forward for the writer. Indeed, the last paragraph reads like a convincing personal creed, a manifesto upon which the writer has committed himself. And it's difficult to believe that he will ever let himself follow another.

—Esther Yi

IV. STORYTELLER: EXPERIENCES THAT ILLUMINATE CHARACTER

Who are you? Sure, you might be captain of the tennis team, a straight-A student, or the lead in the school play. Maybe you have a perfect SAT score or a high school transcript peppered with fives from your AP tests. While the rest of your application will allow you to show the admissions officers your accomplishments, the essay is your chance to show them your character. While not evident in your scores or grades, your perspective, attitude, and personality are important traits that give admissions officers a better picture of who you are and what you would be like as a student.

One way many successful applicants infuse their personality in their application is by writing about an experience that illustrates their character. The following essays exemplify this technique. Regardless of whether the experience these students describe is a significant event or what others would consider an everyday occurrence, each of these essays shows the character of the person behind the application.

Molly Wehlage—"I've Grown Out of It"

I didn't do much crying when I was young.

In the great wide world of the playground, crying and tattling are the two greatest signs of weakness—fatal mistakes that a clever young fourth-grader would never commit. I was a respected teammate on the recess soccer and football teams and the tomboy on the playground—or rather the little girl that adored her school-uniform jumper, hair ribbons, and books, but happened to love sports. Crying, even when a semiflat kickball slams into an unprepared face, didn't earn the respect of my teammates, and it certainly wouldn't help a girl in the cutthroat sports world my male classmates entered at the ringing of the afternoon recess bell.

I learned to be tough and hold my tears.

I distinctly remember one of our rare but highly anticipated family "TV-tray dinner nights" at home. My sister and I were watching a slightly pathetic movie, *All Dogs Go to Heaven*. During a particularly sad part, my little sister, younger by a year and a half, looked over at me from the TV tray next to mine and said with tears in her eight-year-old eyes, "Why aren't you crying?" An uneasiness over my inability to cry distracted me from watching the rest of the movie, but what shook me most was her later conclusion that I possessed a "cold heart."

I have surely changed.

I baby-sit for a family of three girls: four-year-old twins and a nine-month-old. The most recent time I was at the Todd house, the girls picked out a bedtime story (as is the routine); this time, it was *Love You Forever* by Robert Munsch, a story I didn't have to pretend to be excited to read, as the memory of my own mother reading it to me sparked my curiosity. (It was her favorite book; I didn't love it all that much.) As I began reading, I felt like I was back in my parents' king-sized bed listening to my mother's voice tell the story: A new mother, struggling every day with her ornery toddler, enters his room at night while he's fast asleep, rocks him in her arms, and sings him this song: "I'll love you forever, I'll like you for always; as long as I'm living, my baby you'll be." I sang it aloud to the girls in the same tune my mother had made up when I was a little four-year-old girl, their eyes opening wider at what they perhaps naively thought was a pretty singing voice. The story repeats, the mother coming into her son's room at night to rock him in her arms as he grows to be a teenager and even a young man living on his own. The mother calls her son, now a father, to come see her when she is very sick. He drives to his mother's house and takes her aging body into his arms. He sings to the woman about to leave life the same song that the woman who brought him into life always sang to him. After arriving back at his own home and pausing at the top of the stairs for a long time, he enters his new daughter's room, takes her into his arms, and sings to her, "I'll love you forever, I'll like you for always; as long as I'm living, my baby you'll be." The two identical twins looked in my eyes with that earnest four-year-old empathy: "It's okay, don't worry!" We had seemed to switch roles as they reached up to wipe my tears away; I realized I was crying.

Most people think that crying frequently when we're young and then gradually maturing and crying less often is a natural part of growing up. It's been the opposite for me. I don't think crying is a weakness anymore, and although I'm still hesitant to allow people to witness it, the tears come easier than they once did. The girls couldn't understand why I cried while reading that book—to them tears come from a diaper rash, a scrape on the knee, or a broken crayon. It was when I felt my own tears that I realized why my mother loved the book so much. The love of my family is the most important thing in my life, an emotion and a passion that trumps every other. I'm mature enough to realize that now. In a way, tears give us a grounding in life, a solid perspective, an instrument of discovery. Those things that move us to tears, whether sorrowful or joyous, reveal what truly matters to us. The great country I live in that allows me to express these passions is another source of joy in itself. It used to embarrass me that I sometimes cry while watching an American accept a gold medal at the Olympics with his hand over his heart and tears in his eyes, or while listening to an old World War II vet laugh about the "good times" during the war from a wheelchair. I understand now that these tears are a reminder of my pride for my country, our great history, and the fight for liberty. The love of my family and my country will continue to influence my decisions for the rest of my life.

Certainly, strength of character, determination, and emotional control are qualities essential for success. But a simple physical response to a complex emotion should be a blessing to welcome—these tears reveal who we are, what matters most, and what our purpose is in this life. We strive to be tough, but we're human, we cry, and that's okay.

I didn't do much crying when I was young.

I've grown out of it.

COMMENTARY

This writer separates herself from others by embracing an action most people find embarrassing: crying. She approaches the topic in a straightforward manner and clearly walks the reader through her shift from holding back tears to learning to embrace them. She looks beyond the stigma of crying and views the action from a unique perspective, which sheds light on her inner character and thoughtfulness.

While she conquers a unique topic, her concluding points—how her love for her family and country has grown as she has gotten older—are somewhat clumsy. She spends a large part of the essay explaining her personal perspective on crying. However, she doesn't convey her thoughts by example, but through a long, direct explication. Providing examples of her maturity rather than stating it as fact would have made for a much stronger and more concise essay.

Another thing one notices about this essay is its length. At 954 words, the piece is quite long. It likely would have been much more powerful had the writer been more concise. Nevertheless, the writer succeeds in being straightforward without being too simple, an effective communicator who still finds opportune moments to delve deep.

—Kate Leist

Maria Dieci—"The Little Things"

My jaw drops. The drab granite walls on the outside of the cathedral of Sacre Coeur did nothing to prepare me for the luxurious blanket of color that awaited me beyond the heavy wooden doors. The center aisle is filled with tourists, most of whom are snapping photographs of everything in sight, in an attempt to capture the overwhelming beauty of their surroundings. Cautiously, skirting the throng of people, I make my way to the significantly less crowded aisle on the right side of the church. My group, drawn to the striking gold mosaics on the main altar, does not notice my absence. I begin my journey down the hall, each painting and fresco taking my breath away. My footsteps echo in the dimly lit corridor, and I shiver slightly when I touch the cool stone lining the walls. The only light cast on the works of art is that of the sea of offertory candles in front of each one. As I near the end of my tour, out of the corner of my eye I notice a corner with no candles, and immediately assume that it is bare.

If I had been walking a little faster, I surely would have missed it. A lone wooden crucifix, almost swallowed by the dark slate–colored stones on which it hangs. It is made of plain, unpolished wood, sharply in contrast with the rich golds and reds that seem to dominate the rest of the sanctuary. I am immediately pulled toward its simplicity: I can tell that this was not the work of a master. The lines are somewhat jagged, and the measurements are slightly skewed, but what strikes me is the face of the dying Christ. His head, lolling to one side, tells of resignation and defeat. His mouth, pulled taut into a grimace, reveals his pain and suffering. What strikes me the most, however, is the expression in his eyes. Looking toward the heavens, his eyes are not lifeless, but clearly defined, almost sparkling. They hold the promise of hope.

As I gaze on this forgotten treasure, I think about its maker. His unwavering faith is evident in each angle and curve of the carving. I reflect on the time it must have taken to complete even such a simple piece. Did it take weeks? Months? How did it end up in such a cathedral? It seems to me that it is extremely out of place. Whatever the case, I know the artist would not have wanted his work to go unnoticed. My heart goes out to him, as I realize that his devotion and love have been, and will continue to be, overlooked. In a wave of compassion, I find a solitary candle to place at the feet of this ordinary beauty, and light it. The soft glow illuminates the crucifix slightly, making it seem ethereal and holy. Taking special care to capture the subject's poignant expression that echoes the lifetime of affection of the forgotten artist, I take a picture. Now I know that he is no longer alone.

COMMENTARY

This essay details a brief moment during the author's life in which she discovers a simple crucifix in the corner of a cathedral. She does not attempt to wow the reader with the particulars of a volunteer experience or athletic victory. The essay is a chance to show admissions officers the consideration and motivation that surround your actions, and this essay provides the reader insight into the writer's thought process and her awareness of her environment. The reader accompanies the writer through her stream of thoughts while inside the cathedral, from choosing to break away from the larger group to contemplating the identity of the maker of the crucifix.

The strength of the essay lies in its descriptive language. Her vivid descriptions and use of the present tense envelop the reader in the moment. She starts strong with the short but gripping line, "My jaw drops." Her essay leaves out the details of her experience, such as the members of the "group" she was with or why she was visiting the cathedral. Instead, she fills her essay with descriptive lines such as, "It is made of plain, unpolished wood, sharply in contrast with the rich golds and reds that seem to dominate the rest of the sanctuary." These strong illustrative phrases and her detailed recollection of this lone crucifix from a one-time visit to the cathedral demonstrate not only the power of her memory, but also her personality.

After an essay spent separate from contact with others, the writer's attempt to join herself with the artist at the end feels a bit uncomfortable, especially when she expresses pity for the artist. Overall, however, she succeeds at using this experience to convey her willingness to separate from the mainstream in pursuit of her own interests, as well as her ability to notice beauty in items that others overlook.

—Lauren Kiel

ELIZABETH MELLER—"CHARLIE"

I spent much of my freshman year wearing a cape. I didn't don this accessory to foil evil plots of world domination, overcome snarky supervillains, or make a statement at an upperclassmen Halloween party, but to complete my costume as mascot of the Edina Robotics Team.

My sister's friends began the team the summer before my freshman year. As a nosy younger sibling with a keen interest in screwdrivers and power tools, I naturally began to follow her to meetings. I helped market our team to local businesses to gain grants and funds, and I brought my screwdrivers to help build the robot. Unfortunately, the rest of the team intimidated me: They were all much older and bigger, and boys still totally freaked me out. I wanted a stronger role on the team, but I couldn't even work up the nerve to speak.

When competitions began to loom, the team captain made a startling discovery: Our team needed a mascot. Eager to make an impact, I volunteered for the role. Since our team was called "the Green Machine," I became a green metallic superhero. I sported power boots, armlets, a vest, fishnets, a mask, and a gauzy cape that billowed impressively when I walked. Afraid that the homemade outfit couldn't compare to the professional ensembles of other teams' mascots, I packed my green juggling clubs to enhance my image.

At our first competition in Milwaukee, I felt awkward and out of place. I was accustomed to blending into the background, but the overhead lights reflected off my metallic costume, forcing me to stand out. I missed our team's first match because I was petrified to step onto the playing field in my alien garb.

IV. Storyteller: Experiences that Illuminate Character

When our robot was wheeled out for its second match, I stepped gingerly into the field for the introductions. Music that was popular years ago blasted deafeningly from the speakers, and the bleachers surrounding the arena were packed. I squinted into the audience, overwhelmed by the rainbow of teams wearing matching T-shirts, and feebly waved our flag. To my surprise, the audience erupted into applause. In disbelief, I waved the flag again to incite similar results. I thrust the flag and my fist into the air, and my team rose as one and whooped.

Emboldened by this positive response, I gained more confidence with each match. Soon I was dashing about the field with my cape fluttering and gleaming in the light, pumping up the crowd and leading my team in cheers. I brought my clubs to the arena floor with me and whipped out my best juggling tricks (although these were not executed on the playing field—I was very wary of the intricate machinery of the robots). I even worked some crazy dance moves into my routine.

Our final competition was the national championship in Atlanta, Georgia. I couldn't wait to transform into my new alter ego. My journey was only mildly hampered by a mishap in security—I decided to pack my juggling clubs in my carry-on bag, and the guard noticed an uncanny resemblance to weapons. Once I juggled to prove my claim, the whiskered old guard gestured me on with a wink.

I had a new goal for this competition, since one of our mentors had advised us to "cross-fertilize" with the other teams. She meant that we should network and form connections, which I normally would have been much too nervous to attempt. However, amused by the unintended connotations and empowered by my new identity, I was determined to "cross-fertilize" as much as possible. I introduced myself and initiated conversations with members from other teams, and I became fast friends with the other mascots. When I heard that my teammates were competing to gain the most phone numbers, I tried out my best robotics-themed pick-up lines.

By my junior year, my concert band obligations conflicted with the Robotics Build Season, and I had to retire the cape. However, I no longer require my superhero guise; I can now fight off anxiety without superpowers.

COMMENTARY

For this essay, the writer uses an extracurricular experience—in this case, serving as the mascot for the school robotics team—to illuminate a journey of personal growth. She illustrates how she conquered her shyness to become not only an outstanding mascot, but also a more self-confident individual in general.

One of the essay's strengths is its straightforward structure. The narrative is easy to follow, and the writer's purpose is clear. At the beginning, she indicates her goal and describes the weakness that initially holds her back with the line, "I wanted a stronger role on the team, but I couldn't even work up the nerve to speak." The piece would benefit from a more explicit explanation for the author's desire to become more involved and overcome her fear—elements that would have strengthened the otherwise clear message that her experience allowed her to blossom outside of her comfort zone.

Without being too obvious, the writer manages to convey a number of positive personality traits through the account of her experiences. She shows that she is curious (she had a "keen interest in screwdrivers and power tools" as a child), resourceful (she "packed my green juggling clubs" to enhance her homemade outfit), and funny ("I tried out my best robotics-themed pick-up lines"). In essence, the author utilizes her experience to showcase her best and most admirable traits, and she allows readers to see a fuller picture of her by situating herself in action—and not situating herself entirely in description.

The essay's main weakness lies in its writing style. Although the author makes it a point to use colorful, descriptive language, it is often halting and even jerky at parts. Certain word choices and phrases are simply awkward ("However, amused by the unintended connotations and empowered by my new identity, I was determined to 'cross-fertilize' as much as possible"). Furthermore, the abrupt ending leaves readers hanging—if being a mascot was so fulfilling, why did she quit in order to focus more on concert band?

Overall, the essay does not display the most sophisticated ear for language. The writer is successful because she has taken a predictable college essay trope—overcoming a personal obstacle—and given it an offbeat twist, making for an entertaining and enlightening essay.

—Michelle Quach

Yuqing Meng—"Music in the Basement"

The heavy wooden doors slowly inched aside to reveal a dark room. My arms had goose bumps from the cool air; music scores weighed down my backpack. Feeling ready, I took a step into the room just as my teacher snapped on the lights. I was there—the basement of Steinway Hall, the epicenter of twentieth-century classical music. As I passed the nine-foot Steinway pianos, I noticed the portraits of the great masters: Vladimir Horowitz rested his hands on the keys and stared at the black and white organism before him; Rachmaninoff stared at his score with his signature expression of melancholy. Their unfocused gazes suggested deep meditation. What were they thinking about?

I unexpectedly started to perspire. I had not practiced much during the week. For months, I had felt bored sitting in front of the piano for four hours every day. As a four-year-old, I had loved how I could make combinations of sounds just by tinkering with the keys. But by the time I turned fourteen, I no longer saw the point of memorizing so many seemingly random notes and playing music that none of my friends understood. I felt trapped by this imposing machine and could not escape the eternal cycles of practice.

Wiping the perspiration off my forehead, I clenched my jaw and began playing Beethoven's Opus 110 Sonata. Gradually, I sensed that my teacher was living the music. Her hands subtly imitated the motion of the melody, rising and falling like a gentle wave. She must have been imagining the pain that Beethoven had felt at the realization that he was losing the last remnants of his hearing.

She neither flinched nor coughed until the last vestiges of the sonata had disappeared into the dry basement air. As my hands gently came back down onto my lap, she flashed a radiant smile and said, "This piece is perfect for you!" For the next fifty minutes, she focused on the minutest details. She demonstrated that with a slight variation in the motion of the arm, I could make the melody sing more. And just by touching the keys in another place, I could control the left-hand harmonies and vary the warmth of the tone. In other parts of the piece, she played the section multiple times with slight differences in the length of the rests. That extra fraction gave me the chance to breathe along with the music.

As I listened in awe to the numerous nuances in only thirty-one pages of notes, I realized that this was why I started playing the piano so long ago. As a child, I loved exploring the mellifluous sounds, imagining that they were voices and animal calls. I enjoyed creating interpretations of the notes on the page and discovering that subtle relationship between the notes and rests.

I regained my passion for music and exploration.

COMMENTARY

Students probing for college essay topics are often given lists of subjects to avoid at all costs. Don't write about the challenges you faced as captain of the soccer team. Don't write about how you learned all cultures are one through your volunteer efforts in Africa. Don't write about how you bonded with your grandfather when you finally started listening to his stories of walking uphill to school in the snow both ways. (In fact, don't include anybody over sixty-five in your essay at all: It can only slide into sentimentality.) Oh, and for God's sake, don't even think about writing about music— musicians applying to Harvard are a dime a dozen.

With these dictates in mind, writing an essay like this one can be a far riskier proposition than tackling a more obscure or eccentric theme; the chance of something fresh emerging in such a well-mined field can be slim indeed. Happily, this writer manages to pull it off through his vulnerability and warmth of description. An atmospheric introduction sets the tone: A large room in which many of the classical greats have played, a few portraits of said greats, and the writer's own unease at not having practiced for some time are all painted elegantly. We're taken into his mind and into his childhood; his physical discomforts are briefly sketched out. Here, as in the entire essay, sensory impressions are key, especially given that the subject matter is music.

This comes to a head when the writer relates his teacher's total immersion in a Beethoven sonata—it's this immersion that ultimately inspires him to rediscover his own childish joy in making beautiful sounds. Moved by his teacher's playing, the writer—who had been on the cusp of losing his faith in music altogether—finds the inspiration to open himself up to the idea of playing music again. He makes himself vulnerable, willing to embrace the new possibilities of an arena that he thought he had once known.

The essay's flaws nearly all concern slightly awkward choices of word or phrase ("black and white organism"; "imposing machine") that a careful editor could easily remedy. Occasionally, trite expressions ("clenched my jaw"; "flashed a radiant smile"; "listened in awe") fill space in which more evocative description could be imagined; perhaps the old chestnut "show, don't tell" would find application here. And the one-sentence ending seems overly abrupt after the past few hundred words of intricate reverie.

But these faults (again, quite fixable ones) are outweighed by the writer's tenderness in describing his teacher and his own apprehensions. In the end, this vulnerability is what makes the piece successful. When writing a college essay, the natural first inclination is to describe only one's strengths: What better way to present oneself than in the best light possible? Too often, though, this can turn into mere bragging or a laundry list of achievements. This piece avoids that pitfall by taking the opposite tack: By revealing the author's anxieties, it arouses a much deeper sympathy in the reader than any mention of his no-doubt formidable musical honors ever could.

—Jessica Sequeira

Jackie Hsieh—"There Were No Tears"

At the age of four, I started Chinese school by proclaiming that I would simultaneously give up my baby bottle. Thus began the road to maturity. Paralleled by the study of American literature in school, I began analyzing Chinese language and folklore. Yet, despite spending a lifetime absorbing both cultures, it was in the summer of 2003 that a decade of memorizing Chinese characters, idioms, and poetry truly had meaning.

I was standing in a small storage room, pointing to a cracking blackboard. I glanced at my eager students; these were not the typical rowdy children you'd expect a teenager to teach. Instead, they were attentive senior citizens trying to learn English. "American citizen," I articulated slowly for the tenth time. "Now repeat after me."

These were Chinese grandmothers, grandfathers, aunts, and uncles who had immigrated to America and were hoping for the citizenship of their dreams. After class, many of them would seek me out, narrating their stories of hardship—first struggling to do so in English, then finishing off in Chinese. I felt like a granddaughter being told of her ancient grandparents' journey to a new life. From their stories, I gathered a richness of culture weaved into the words.

They honored me with these stories to thank me for my patience in repeating simple English for them to understand. They told me of their sadness from having Chinese-American grandchildren who had never learned Chinese or even understood the culture from which they were born. It was a blessing, they said, that a girl born and raised in America could still understand their stories and the world they had come from.

Yet, during that summer, I had not completely understood the strength of language until an evening shift volunteering at New York Hospital Queens. It was an evening that proved to be more than quotidian clerical duties.

An announcement blared over the intercom: "This is an emergency! We need someone who speaks Mandarin in the isolation room immediately!" I perked my head up and looked toward the isolation room. Amidst the busy background noise of conversations and mechanical beeps, I could make out an anguished scream. I could not even hesitate at the thought of the man's pain. I headed toward the room without realizing I'd never been in contact with a patient.

The man lying on the bed was screaming what must have sounded like a jumble of nonsensical words. That jumble was his story. "This is Mr. Wong," the nurse said, but I wasn't listening. My ears were only hearing the words of the patient and my eyes were only seeing the fright in his eyes. There were no tears.

I spit an English translation from my mouth as Mr. Wong's words narrated the cause of his pains. The doctor set to work once he understood. I soothed Mr. Wong, "Mister, you'll be okay now."

There were tears. His fear had melted within his eyes. *"Tian shr,"* he said. *Angel.*

At that point I understood the power of language.

COMMENTARY

This piece edges toward one of the scourges of college application essays, self-aggrandizement, but the writer tempers that tendency by framing the major events as a learning process she underwent, rather than good deeds performed.

This essay gives the reader a sense of the writer's background without actually focusing on the circumstances of her upbringing. We don't need to be told explicitly that she has a close connection to the Chinese immigrant community; instead, we see how that connection has influenced important moments in her life. More broadly, this essay demonstrates her values—compassion, an interest in social service—in a genuine, tangible way.

Helping to save a life is obviously unique, but the writer turns that event into a personal epiphany related to a lifelong inquiry. She makes three disparate incidents into a coherent narrative with the consistent theme "the strength of language." She eschews unnecessary detail in favor of powerfully evocative phrasing. The occasional stilted phrase holds this essay back; be sure to read yours aloud a few times and edit for smoothness.

—Sarah Howland

Danielle O'Neil—"Coming Home"

My family has never been one for convention. On the last day of school in fifth grade, my father picked me up in his latest junkyard acquisition—an old fire truck. To my preteen self, this, and almost every aspect of my family, seemed disturbingly "uncool," and contradicted what I thought American suburbia was supposed to be like. Our lawn was untamed and housed the humiliating fire truck. Instead of a picket fence and a garden, we had a totem pole and a dilapidated barn that was older than our house. Although I loved my family and the time we spent outdoors, I had a nagging feeling that because of our lifestyle, I was missing out on the stereotypical suburban experience that was a common ground for my peers.

My embarrassment reached an entirely new level in high school. My dad achieved near-celebrity status for wearing a purple cape to every football game. My friends had pools and movie theaters at home; I avoided having guests because of our lack thereof. Even my house itself was unconventional compared to the vinyl-sided abodes of my friends, all within the confines of suburbia. An old, wooden building, it slumbered at the edge of a valley. Bordered by the languid Meramec River and an expanse of warm grasses and Missouri wildflowers, it was an isolation camp. It wasn't home per se—home was with my family. There was no attachment to what had kept me from a "normal" suburban life.

It was spring of my junior year, and my mom and I were visiting colleges when we received word that our lazy neighbor, the Meramec River, was flooding at record-setting pace. My dad and sister were moving everything, including the fire truck, to safety. We arrived to the sight of the valley filled with angry water, the house a lonely island in a raging display of raw natural power.

My dad and I went to the house to assess the damage before the water crested. The roads I was accustomed to driving served as both a launching point and a path for our boat. Venturing into the flood was surreal; the valley I had known my entire life was sickeningly empty. I could identify neighbors' homes, barns, and mailboxes—but they were different. The presence of the floodwaters betrayed my memory and the comfort that came with living there my entire life.

Halfway to the house the engine on our small boat died. I frantically groped for a telephone pole, clinging to it desperately while my dad cleared the grass that had accumulated in the engine, halting our progress. Drifting into the trees would be lethal in the fast current. The laziness of my lifetime neighbor was forgotten in the face of the violent water that seemed determined to engulf us.

As I clung to the pole, I had a clear view of my house. Its profusion of windows was dark and sullen; hay bales floated by determinedly. I couldn't believe it: The despondency of my home saddened me. Seeing it empty bridged the gap I had felt between the concepts of house and home. My best memories originated in that house; seeing it in danger frightened me. I was grateful that my family didn't have a manicured lawn in suburbia. I was grateful for the wilderness that surrounded us. I was grateful, most of all, for my family's tolerance of my embarrassment. My family, eccentricities and all, allowed me to become who I am, encouraged my pursuits, and showed me things that I never would have fathomed in a vinyl-sided house, all while dealing with a daughter who was naïve enough to wish for a picket fence.

When the engine roared back to life, I let go of the pole. I couldn't help but smile at my house's large, brooding windows; I know it was a trick of the light, but I like to think they winked at me. I was coming to save my house, my home, after years of denial. I was embracing my childhood, seizing my future and the unique experiences that shaped me, and I loved it. I was proud of my family, their faith in me, and that I shed the burden of suburban expectations. I was excited to show my gratitude to them by achieving the dreams that they had supported and nourished. I had a lifetime of experiences that I could carry with me like pleasant secrets from the world of suburbia that had relished my status as an outsider as I faced the real world. By winking, my house was forgiving me, laughing away my childlike naïveté. I was excited for my future and everything that it would bring, all thanks to my wood-sided cabin among the trees.

COMMENTARY

This essay is a layered narrative that draws the reader into the writer's world and mind-set. First, there is the overarching story of her changing feelings about her house, which serves as a microcosm of her feelings about her family's eccentricity. Second, there is the more detailed, exciting, and powerfully emotional story of the flood—a distinct turning point that clearly marks the writer's changed attitude. Finally, the images the student uses become sharper as she transitions from hazily describing an imagined suburban utopia to cleanly evoking her beloved home and the river that flows past it. This subtle narrative in the author's evolving voice is difficult to pull off—it is hard for readers to distinguish between unintentional and stylistic vagueness—but it can be an artful way of evoking your thought process.

Instead of simply laying out the events of the flood, the author wisely chooses to focus the reader's attention on the way the flood affected her outlook. She drives this focus home with the repeated statement "I was grateful," in the second-to-last paragraph; the reader can understand how profound this moment was for her. Furthermore, she identifies a single, symbolic focal point for her changed outlook: the house. This decision gives her space for lots of whimsical details about the house, whereas if she tried to cram in too many examples of how odd her family is, there would not have been room in the essay to fully flesh out any of them.

This piece could be cleaned up with a smoother transition from the background about the family's eccentricity to the narrative of the flood, and by cutting out words and phrases like "abode" and "profusion of windows" that clash with the relaxed tone of most of the piece. Establishing a consistent mood in your essay can be an organic way of letting the admissions office see your unique personality. You can do this by experimenting with the structure of the essay as a whole (break free of the traditional five paragraphs), the scale and order of the narrative, and/or the tone in which you present it. Whatever decisions you make about style, commit to them, so that the final product reads as a coherent piece of writing, rather than a series of experiments. Each fully realized stylistic choice reflects something about who you are—and who you want to become in college.

—Sarah Howland

Stephanie McCartney—"A Beach Game"

My sister holds the small, maroon pouch out to me and shakes it back and forth. "Pick a blank, Steph; we need a blank," she whispers. I snatch three letters. No blank. It is my father's turn, and we are all anticipating another perfectly placed gem. My sister and I watch as he configures and reconfigures his tiles, while my younger brother climbs up on his back. Then my dad makes his move. Cocking his head to the side, smiling wilily, he places all seven of his letters onto the board one by one, pausing dramatically between each click. "And I believe that gives me," he counts, touching the surface of each letter, "ahh . . . seventy-three points." He doesn't wait for us to ask him how he does it. "It's all about placement," he brags amusedly, "and brains." Winking at my little brother, he adds, "Now, pick me some more winners, Joe."

In our playful rivalries, my dad has always been invincible: unbeatable when we would play board games, uncatchable when we would sprint around our basement playing cat-and-mouse, and unconquerable in arguments. Even when I held my own in a discussion, my dad would claim victory. "Aha," he would proclaim with that wry smile, "I've taught you well." And just like that, even though he had lost, he had won.

To this day, I seek out my father's challenges. My dad has always been there as a loving rival. Beating him is different from beating my mom, my sister, or my friends. When I compete against my dad and win, I want to dance, to sing, and, yes, to gloat. Because my dad is such a worthy adversary, I always want to play, race, and argue again and again. Without my knowing it, my father has used every competition as a teaching moment.

Among his many lessons, my dad has taught me to never give up. When I transitioned from the junior varsity to the varsity soccer team my junior year, I competed with girls who could kick harder, dribble quicker, and sprint faster than I could. Even worse, during games, I was left watching as my teammates took the field. I realized I had to do something to improve. I began juggling in my driveway, dribbling in my backyard, and volleying in the kitchen with my sister. By the time the following soccer season arrived, I was ready, and was gratified that some of my teammates noticed the difference. I could have quit, but the competitive spirit my dad nurtured in me told me that quitting was not an option.

Working with the same letters, my sister and I struggle to discover a winning word. Suddenly, I realize I can merge our A, S, and E with a W and T already on the board to make WASTE—double word score. My dad will appreciate the elegance of the move, even though the word is worth thirty-two fewer points than his last turn. "Jackie! I've got one!" Giggling, my sister and I slap hands and watch as our father records our points onto the tally sheet. "See, Dad?" I say after a moment, "It's all about placement and brains." He grins with pride.

COMMENTARY

The author's essay is a well-organized piece of writing, and it comes full circle nicely. The recurring quote, "It's all about placement and brains," unifies the essay around a central theme: The phrase is spoken by the author's father as a mantra to live by, and it is repeated yet again by the author to demonstrate that she has learned to live according to the ideals established by her father. The phrase's first appearance comes in the context of her father's victory, but by the time the author repeats it, the quote does not register within the same context. Rather, its repetition displays that she has made progress, that she possesses a positive, optimistic attitude. She communicates that it is her spirit and outlook—instead of her simple achievements—that are ultimately important in the shaping of her character.

The writer frames her persistence and her competitive relationship with her father within an anecdote about a game of Scrabble. She then employs the example of her transition from the JV to varsity soccer team to demonstrate how her competition with her father has become a positive force in her life and motivates her to succeed. Although this essay has a clear message, its structure and overall tone are perhaps a bit too generic and lack a clear personality to fully distinguish it from the thousands of other application essays the admissions officer must read.

Overall, however, this is a solid essay that could be improved by making it more specific to the author and by narrowing the topic such that the allotted space is adequate to explore it.

—Sarah Joe Wolansky

Amy Sun—"Beauty in a Potbelly"

I sat in a worn wooden chair in front of the mahogany easel. My legs, not yet long enough to reach the floor, swung back and forth with impatience. I gripped the pencil in my hand. I could not wait to become an artist. What would I draw? Beautiful landscapes of the setting sun? Portraits of mysterious women? A whole table full of fresh fruit and golden goblets? I heard the slow *boom-cha, boom-cha* of my art teacher walking slowly into the room, wearing slippers and carrying a cup of tea in one hand. In his other hand, he held a rusty pot. He placed it on the table in front of me.

"Draw this," he said as he sipped the tea.

"What?" I was dumbfounded. There was nothing special about this pot, no magic. It was just an old piece of junk, blackened and sooty from the burner with a handle slightly bent out of shape. "I want to draw something pretty!" I whined.

"You don't think that this pot is pretty?" my art teacher replied, his face serious. I didn't know whether or not to laugh; I just shook my head no. He did not reply. Instead, he turned around and pulled a book from the top of his shelf. It was a catalog of paintings that he opened and handed to me.

"Look at this."

I looked where he pointed with curiosity. It was an old, realistic oil painting with a dark background. The painting portrayed overturned goblets of wine, some rotting fruit, and a piece of stale bread. It was sublime.

"Do you see how the artist painted the crust of the bread? You can almost touch it. And look here, at the color of the rust on the pot."

I scrutinized the details of the painting, even running my fingers along the two-dimensional objects. I nodded.

"Do you think this painting is ugly?" he asked.

"No." I leaned back in my seat, embarrassed. I looked at the saucepan I was to draw, but as if by magic, it had changed. I now noticed the way the metal body of the pot bunched up where the handle was bent in shapely ridges, how the blackness from the bottom crept up the burnished sides like wisps of smoke. I noticed the pale orange mixed with the light brown of rust. At last, I glimpsed its hidden charm. It was as if I had discovered access to a new world, and the only way I could share it was to render it on the blank page before me.

Over the years, I have sketched and painted countless old pots and common vegetables, as well as a fair share of embellished china and autumn foliage. I found that one subject is not superior to another, but rather, that I was misguided in presuming that only clean, delicate objects could make beautiful art. In fact, some of my favorite pieces of my own work are renderings of unconventional objects. When I finally saw beyond my preconceptions of beauty, the real soul of my subject was revealed to me. I realized that just as the shabbiest objects can become the subject of the most exquisite paintings, and the most run-down pizzerias can serve the best calzones, true insight can come from the most unexpected of places.

COMMENTARY

Hobbies and individual passions are popular essay topics that can hold much potential, as they often provide an opportunity to expound on what isn't readily apparent from two lines on a résumé.

The essay's strength lies in the honest portrayal of the author's skewed perception of what she had considered art. She acknowledges her initial failure to appreciate the wisdom of her art teacher's instruction. The rusty pot her teacher places before her holds "no magic" in her inexperienced eyes. But the author readily admits her error in judging the pot too hastily and recounts through vivid examples the beauty that lies in a painting of overturned goblets of wine and rotting fruit. She takes the reader through her new perspective as she examines the intricacies and nuances in a saucepan.

The author not only showcases her passion and dedication to painting but also takes a simple conversation with her art teacher to highlight a lesson learned.

—June Wu

V. THROUGH THEIR EYES: FINDING YOURSELF IN OTHERS

The idea of writing a personal essay that focuses on anyone except the author may sound like a paradoxical task that only brings the applicant closer to the rejection pile. After all, isn't the college essay one of the few opportunities the author has to further enliven an individual that has been hitherto restricted to a couple of statistics and recommendations? As the following essays demonstrate, however, there is a fine art to writing about others in order to reveal the deepest and most fragile parts of an author—and often, those inner gems can make all the difference in the creation of the most honest and compelling essay possible. As you will see, the following applicants succeed because they use an outside individual to draw attention to some significant portion of their own character. Indeed, it often escapes our minds that some of the most revealing elements of a given individual are the relationships that he or she holds close to heart, those moments of bliss, rapture, and even suffering that arise from the simple fact that humans interact and connect.

So, if you decide to write an essay that focuses on a family member, a friend, or a mentor close to you—or perhaps even a complete stranger—remember to use that individual as a vehicle through which you deepen the reader's understanding of your own complexities.

Joe Sullivan—"Elephant Daddy"

1996

The appointed hour approaches. I crouch anxiously behind the door. He arrives. Like a cheetah pouncing on its prey, I tense every muscle in my body as I leap onto his torso and cling on desperately. Boiling with emotion, I scream, "Elephant Daddy!" My victim and I start gushing with laughter, buzzing with giggles as he carries an elated six-year-old on his back like an elephant. Though it signals the conclusion of the favorite part of my day, I am as content as can be as I plod onto the couch and the ride draws to a close.

Soon he reemerges, taking a seat at the kitchen table. I prance over to join him, my sister, and my mom for dinner. Elephant Dad's postdinner activities are varied. They might include a duel with a small, blond-haired Lancelot wielding a plastic sword in the employ of King Arthur, or a History Channel documentary with an impressionable little boy lying snugly across his body, soothed by the gentle rise and fall of his chest, comforted by the steady rhythm of his heart.

2008

The last in the house to go to bed, my father and I are snacking on mint–chocolate chip ice cream over the kitchen table as the clock strikes midnight. We share stories about the day that has passed and plans for the day that will be, intermittently swapping bits of advice and pieces of encouragement. At times we are serious and concerned. At times we are burning off the calories from the ice cream as we laugh the visceral, belly-based laugh common to us both. All this time, though, we are relishing our time together. Just like we did twelve years ago at that same table, just like we will for as long as life and circumstance allow.

Many of my friends say their father has influenced them by pushing them to run the proverbial extra mile en route to some generic, idealized form of success. But not my daddy. His constant and unwavering supply of tender attention has not only given me the confidence to pursue whatever dreams waltz into my mind, but to stay level-headed and to take life in jest, in stride. If Shakespeare was right when he said, "All the world is a stage/And all the men and women merely players," my father has taught me to stay humble and collected amid tragedy and triumph alike, to smile at the end of each scene.

While his spine doesn't enjoy all 215 pounds of my company, I don't consider it an anachronism when I continue to refer to my father as "Elephant Dad." For in many cultures, the elephant is a symbol of sagacity, a creature with a reservoir of wisdom between its flopping ears. And now, as I prepare to leave my home of eighteen years, I realize all the beautiful lessons Elephant Dad has taught me, lessons he somehow managed to sew into the fabric of my most cherished, emotional childhood memories.

COMMENTARY

This applicant has the distinction of having written two of the essays included in this book. The first, "untitled," is philosophical. The second, presented here, is sweet without being cloying or egocentric. Taken together, these essays demonstrate to any admissions officer that he is a talented, multifaceted writer.

V. Through Their Eyes: Finding Yourself in Others

The writer takes risks in this piece, and they pay off. He writes about deeply felt but not particularly dramatic emotions, describing in reverent detail an ongoing relationship rather than a single significant moment. He plays with the essay format, presenting two related images separated by dates, without formally tying them together. The reader can tell from the articulate, clean writing that the unusual format is experimentation, rather than sloppiness. Plus, in a forum where most writers work hard to demonstrate their maturity, he admits that he still calls his father "Daddy."

The author establishes a tender, nostalgic tone and focuses on the domestic warmth that his father has imparted to him, rather than a more tangible skill or drive to succeed. The writer makes this work by providing many specific, artfully described examples of what makes his relationship with his father so special. Furthermore, he maintains a wide-eyed admiration of his father even in the present-day section of the essay, avoiding the temptation to shrug off a "childish" mood. Instead, this applicant artfully demonstrates his development with the mature phrase "plans for the day that will be" and an original treatment of an overused quote. The consistent atmosphere reinforces his thesis that a close relationship with his father has helped him develop into a sturdy young man.

—Sarah Howland

DEVON SHERMAN—"RUNNING WITH FOUR FEET"

Mud and dusty gravel grind beneath our gleaming back-to-school sneakers. Encroaching weeds have long eroded the edges of the old track but it appears as an Olympic stadium. My identical twin sister, Elise, occupies the lane next to me. With shared anxiety and shaking knees, we take a visual trip around the endless course. Our first timed mile is about to begin.

Lap One, 0:00 minutes:

In the midst of my anticipation, the whistle blows. Elise sprints ahead, leaving me on the starting line.

With frozen legs, I detect the distinct smell of new crayons as I stare up at an ominous sign, which reads, MRS. PILACHOWSKI'S FIRST GRADE CLASSROOM. The paper apples that border the door envelop me like my older brother's torturous headlock. Giggling among a crowd of students, Elise breezes into the classroom across the hall and slaps on her name tag. How can I enter without my identical twin sister, my second half?

The race is bound to start so I open the door. Will anyone know that there are two people on this track, running different races?

Lap Two, 1:49 minutes:

I take shorter steps and pump my arms more rigorously than Elise.

Friends, teachers, and coaches bombard us with monotonous

questions. "Elise or Devon? Which one are you? Do you have the same dreams each night?" Unable to effectively articulate their curiosity, most people cannot fully grasp what it is like to have an identical twin. As I grow older, my individuality yearns to be released as fervently as an innocent man wrongfully accused. I am a risk taker who craves fajitas with hot peppers while Elise is a perfectionist who will venture no further than a cheeseburger. I am a math nut with negligent penmanship rather than a literature lover who meticulously dots her *i*'s.

The spectators surrounding the track, however, only see that we are wearing the same orange Nike sneakers and that our hair curls more on the right side of our heads. Is running backward the only way to prove my independence?

Lap Three, 3:01 minutes:

Fatigue sets in.

I have an arduous day during which I lose my Latin homework, trip down the gym stairs, and miss an open net in my soccer match. My breathing resembles that of an eighty-year-old man trudging up the Eiffel Tower. "Keep it up, Dev, we're almost done!" encourages Elise. My homework is found. My balance is restored. My shot is buried.

Ample motivation drips off of me along with the sweat running down my forehead. I am as fast, if not faster than my sister, and the track is no longer endless.

Lap Four, 4:52 minutes:

I gain on Elise until we are shoulder to shoulder. The clock is obsolete for we are one another's pacesetters.

I ace a grueling calculus test and we rejoice. Elise backs our '94 Explorer into the garage and we share the guilt. My triumph is her gain. Her failure is my loss. I run my own race but it feels as if I have four feet to carry me.

The end is visible. Accelerating into a sprint, I lead Elise. Alone, I am fully capable; together, we are relentless.

Finish, 6:00 minutes:

With shared exhilaration and aching muscles, we simultaneously cross the finish line.

Having restored my stamina, I stand atop the podium. Supported by my spare set of feet, I stride into the classroom. My twin sister, my pacesetter, my trophy stands beside me. Our individuality has been freed but our friendship is forever bonded.

A knowing smile, a humble glance, and we are off for another lap.

COMMENTARY

Having an identical twin brother or sister is not that common, and neither are narratives as successful as this essay. The author tells her story creatively, while she relays how she perceives herself as an identical twin.

The framing of her essay is creative. Breaking her thoughts by laps allows the writer to provide momentary glimpses into her life: Just as the laps of a run join together to total a mile, these anecdotes join together to tell one larger story about her relationship with Elise. She vividly depicts her mind-set at the onset of the mile and humorously introduces the differences between Elise and her as

V. Through Their Eyes: Finding Yourself in Others

well as the sense of unity she has with her sister. The developments in both her race and her flashbacks chronicle how the author defines her relationship with her twin as she matures.

One of this essay's greatest strengths lies in the writer's humility, in her ability to identify her faults. The essay is a realistic portrayal of her growth, as she is willing to take on responsibilities, learn from her mistakes, and be at peace with who she is.

—Naveen Srivatsa

Ben Biran—"Fruitful Collisions"

At the age of seventy-two, all Safta* Sarah dreamed of was Borowiki mushrooms from her hometown, located on the Polish side of the Lithuanian border. Despite being her fondest wish for over sixty-five years, these extraordinary mushrooms were never enough to make her return to the birthplace she had left during the Holocaust.

Just like Safta Sarah, Meme† longed for some of the unique truffle mushrooms she had back in Casablanca, Morocco. From time to time, she would tell me how she used to anticipate two specific weeks all year long, during which she could seek the underground mushrooms with her father.

Apart from each craving her homeland's mushrooms, seemingly, Meme and Safta Sarah had little in common. Safta was a survivor of the death camps, having escaped the Nazi horrors of the Second World War to find refuge in Israel, after losing most of her family in Europe. Meme was brought up as a religious Moroccan girl and left a prosperous life to fulfill her dream of living in the Holy Land.

These two women had almost nothing in common—other than me, of course. Both were my grandmothers, who equally passed along their cultures to me. Unfortunately, they also sought to define themselves in opposition to one another.

It was never easy growing up as a hybrid. In spite of my parents' disapproval, my grandparents resolutely harbored their cultural dif-

---

*Safta—Grandmother (Hebrew)
†Meme—Grandmother (French)

ferences. Resentful remarks, ethnocentric views of the other, and impatience to native customs were often expressed in my presence. In fact, it seemed quite probable that my grandparents never liked the idea of my parents getting married in the first place.

Growing up, I felt as if I belonged to no one. "Neither!" would be my reply when asked whether I was Sephardic* or Ashkenazi.[†] I was "too Polish" to be called Moroccan and "too Moroccan" to be called Polish.

The day of my Bar Mitzvah changed everything. As the cantor of his Sephardic synagogue, Pepe[‡] was proud to prepare me for my Bar Mitzvah. It was important for him, as an orthodox Jew, that the ceremony be held in the traditional way he had known, in his own Moroccan style. After much preparation and anxious anticipation the day had arrived; all the family was gathered in Pepe's synagogue for my Bar Mitzvah, including Saba[§] Shlomo and Safta Sarah. When the ceremony was over and the synagogue emptied, I noticed Saba Shlomo standing in a corner with a paper in his hand. As I approached him I could tell he had tears in his eyes. I took the paper from his hands: It was a poster that read, *FOLLOW G-D'S ORDERS. THE HOLOCAUST WAS A PUNISHMENT FOR THE JEWS FOR NOT DOING SO.* I knew why Saba Shlomo was crying: He had lost his mother, his six brothers, and his sister in the Holocaust when he was only eight years old.

It was the only time I had seen him cry. I felt ashamed that my grandfather was hurt by my own family. After all, it was Pepe's syna-

---

*Sephardic—Jewish people who immigrated to Israel from the Middle East and the Mediterranean.

[†] Ashkenazi—Jewish people who immigrated to Israel from Central and Eastern Europe.

[‡] Pepe—Grandfather (French)

[§] Saba—Grandfather (Hebrew)

gogue, on the occasion of my Bar Mitzvah. I took the paper and ran outside to find Pepe. I was already crying when I gave him the poster, asking him if he really thought that, since Saba Shlomo's family was murdered by the Nazis. Pepe's face turned white and he rushed to find Saba Shlomo. A few days later, my father told me that Pepe removed all of the posters from his synagogue and decided to quit. He began praying at a new synagogue, but was never a cantor in it. Pepe discovered that some of his best friends were responsible for the posters. He was a courageous man who gave up his greatest passion, cantoring, for his inner truth.

Two years later, Saba Shlomo died of lung cancer. On that year, for the first time, Pepe and Meme invited Safta Sarah to join their side of the family for Passover dinner. It took me a few good minutes of staring at the table to figure out what was so strange about it, until I realized that Meme's Moroccan saffron dish was right next to Safta's Polish gefilte fish. Being the hybrid child that I was, it was touching for me to see how Meme and Pepe embraced Safta and her traditional dishes on the occasion of a holiday dinner. Ashkenazi and Sephardi cultures, in their collision, both assumed leading roles in the history of my country. In the course of the development of my identity, life circumstances, human emotion, and empathy have brought these cultures to an appreciative coexistence. My grandparents decided to let go of their anger and resentment, and learned to love each other. Finally, at the age of fifteen, as this love materialized, my identity fell into place.

Ever since, I would introduce myself as a "fruitful collision" to those curious about my origin. I was the proud Sephardic boy who would say "Oy vey" when he dropped his sandwich, and the Polish student who could speak the best Arabic in class and even spice it up with some Moroccan slang words.

As I grew up, I continued my exploration of culture and identity. At the age of seventeen, I took a trip to Poland to explore my East

European roots. I visited the death camps of Treblinka, Majdanek, and Auschwitz-Birkenau. At a market in the town of Zakopane, I spotted an old lady standing behind a table with large piles of various vegetables for sale. As I closely examined the goods, I noticed large and dark mushrooms I had never seen before. "What are the odds?" I thought. Pointing at the mushrooms: "Borowiki?" I asked. The old lady muttered a few words in Polish and nodded her head in agreement. I picked out the finest mushrooms and carefully wrapped them with newspaper I had in my bag. I paid the old lady and stowed the packet inside my bag, right above my Israeli passport. It was only when I turned away from the stand that a strange idea cropped up in my mind and made me return. "Another few, please," I asked the old Polish lady, pointing at the pile of mushrooms before me. The look on her face made me wish I knew enough Polish to explain I just wanted to get some more for my Meme, for she had never seen these mushrooms back in North Africa, where she was brought up. As I walked back, making my way through the lambs of Zakopane, I could not help but wonder what Moroccan kuskus would taste like with Borowiki mushrooms. "This must be a fruitful collision too," I thought. After all, its ingredients were just like mine.

COMMENTARY

This applicant uses a clever structure to approach a popular essay topic: the challenge of living with a hybrid identity and coming to terms with a cultural duality. The writer begins with a dual perspective on two unidentified women, building suspense until it is revealed that they are both his grandmothers. Furthermore, the author frames his narrative with specific language. His use of cultural terms like the Hebrew word for grandmother ("Safta") and the Polish name for a variety of mushroom ("Borowiki") injects color into his story, and the author lets the story speak for itself. He does not impose the cultural references onto the reader; rather, he allows the terms and colors to imbue the piece with a natural hue that he himself is familiar with.

This essay would benefit from smoother transitions, tighter structuring, and brevity. The author, for example, devotes five paragraphs to describing a culturally rooted conflict between his two grandmothers—too much text can bog down the pace and dampen the effectiveness of an essay. If the author had cut interesting but irrelevant descriptors, the essay's argument would have been more concise.

The opening mushroom anecdote and its reprise at the end is an example of how to place compelling bookends on an essay. The distinctive anecdote emphasizes the cultural rift between two sides of the author's family and constructs a framework for the content of the essay, and the return of the anecdote shows the conflict's resolution and implications for the author's personal growth.

—Monica Liu

Joe Masterman—"Drops"

Water raced across the car windows as we pushed through the summer rain. My head buzzing against the glass, I watched drops of liquid personality race to the edge of the windowpane.

Just over my shoulder, my father was reading his newest "assignment," the same sort of thing he's put me through since I could first speak.

His industry on my behalf is unceasing, often welcome, occasionally tedious and annoying. That day, I thought I was glad for it. Glad that he has kept such a consistent interest in my life, my wellbeing, my future. Glad that he genuinely does want to help.

He looked up, shifting the list to where I could see it. We discussed my answers. After reading the last one aloud, he paused. His eyes seemed strained, almost concerned.

"And I guess this one was a joke?"

His assignment was to write five things I wanted to gain from college. For the last one, I had written "chances to feel educated."

His question cut me and clotted my throat. I felt defensive, hurt. His frankness made me think there was some obvious fact about education I had missed. I felt foolish, as if my vision of college were just some ridiculous fantasy.

He waited for me to say yes. I didn't want to disagree with those earnest blue eyes, but I didn't agree with them, either. After a moment, a mangled sound escaped me, and my eyes found the window again.

The droplets of water were of different sizes, speeds, and paths.

Sometimes their paths crossed, and they collided. Sometimes they simply drifted apart.

I love my father, but we have two very different minds. His is not wrong, but it looks for the next bullet point on the résumé, the classes that yield an extra zero on the paycheck. He is focused and persevering, but he views knowledge—and, largely, the world—as a utility function.

I felt my father hold me in his gaze for a moment longer before shifting his eyes back to the road. "I mean, that's not really a defining goal. That's something that'll just come." He realized he had hurt me, but he wasn't sure how. After all, knowledge is only worth gaining if it is practical, and profitable.

As for me, I love the mind. I want to think, to learn, to understand. The themes of literature, connections of history, nuances of politics and law—these are what truly excite me. I find the feeling of growing, exploring, pursuing, and satiating my mind's appetite, both beautiful and empowering. I had been completely serious about what I had written.

I was torn between my appreciation for my father and my understanding of our differences. His words trickled through my head as I watched the water on the glass.

My father and I both want the same thing: the best for me. We just have quite different ideas of how that will come about. He and I, the drops on the window, we have our own paths. We converge. We diverge. We converge again.

There is something to what my father said. I will not be driven by mere economic gain, but I won't be cavalier about what I do, either. Though I don't completely agree with him, I can appreciate and embrace his discipline and sense of plan. It's not a race to the end. It's a journey. And no one path can get me all the way there by itself.

I looked at him until he looked back at me. Then, I took the list from his hand and asked, "So, what would you suggest for a goal?"

V. Through Their Eyes: Finding Yourself in Others

I won't change my views merely to appease my father, or anyone. But still, for him and for me, I'll see what he has to say.

COMMENTARY

This essay gives life to a subject with which a number of high-achieving applicants are familiar—overbearing parents—and gives it new life. The author talks about his father in frank but forgiving terms, and his delicate handling of a difficult situation conveys a great deal of maturity and poise. To this end, his format of weaving a far-ranging analysis into a small anecdote helps him a great deal.

Many students have felt excessive parental pressure in some regard during their adolescence. However, this author avoids becoming trite by focusing his essay on his father's personality. The author clearly disagrees with his father's perspective, but he doesn't turn this essay into a harangue. Instead, he probes deeply into the reasons behind his father's vigilance, and comes to acknowledge what he believes are legitimate but individual rationales behind his actions. The analogy of converging and diverging drops works well here.

Another one of this essay's strengths is its honesty. It doesn't feel calculated, primarily because it looks at a large situation through the lens of a small anecdote. Instead of making an overt argument for being his own person or for intellectualism, which might seem forced, the author discusses these subjects at logical points in the anecdote.

—Anita Joseph

Tyler Logigian—"Minga"

For as long as I can remember, I've called my grandmother "Minga." Friends often ask if the derivation of this name is Polish, because Minga's ancestors all hail from Poland, but I end up comically explaining to them that somehow in the process of trying to say "Grandma" as a toddler, "Minga" was the best I could muster. There's much more to Minga than her unique name: She's been a fixture through every stage of my life, from pushing the name "Tyler" ahead of my mom's preferred choices to accompanying me on college visits.

Growing up as Minga's grandson has been quite the learning experience; I've helped her make pierogies and other Polish dishes and accompanied her to Bingo at her church. For years, I'd spend part of every weekend at her house. I'd crown myself king of castles that I'd build in her living room, shoot basketballs on her dead-end street, and play poker with her as I dreamed of becoming the clever, fun-loving, risk-taking card shark that I saw in her. These weekend adventures allowed me to develop into the imaginative, "dream big" kind of guy that I am today. In those days, my dreams consisted of building a fort or a castle so gigantic that it blocked Minga's front door; today, my dreams consist of constructing a school playground and a baseball field in an impoverished community in Nicaragua.

A large part of my personal philosophy has been formed by Minga's constant reminder: "God never closes a door without opening a window." Although I've learned that squeezing through an open window might not be as easy as strolling through an open door, I've always found windows large enough to squeeze through in the midst of personal challenges: my mom's struggle with cancer, my parents' pending divorce, and my adjustment to a new school district just before starting high school.

Thanks to Minga's tales of growing up poor, I have a deep sense of gratitude and appreciation for the privileges I enjoy. Minga's emphasis on the importance of compassion helped me develop a personal need to get out into the community. When I came home from my first trip to a local orphanage, Minga was waiting with a hot meal and questions. I passionately explained how I thought I had stumbled across a personal gold mine: self-fulfillment and a place to actualize my passion.

These initial thoughts were quickly confirmed, and I cannot imagine my life without defining myself as a humanitarian. Whenever I return from a trip to Nicaragua, I sit down with Minga and enjoy a precious exchange. As I discuss the needs of the underprivileged with her, I appreciate the connection between her experiences growing up as one of ten kids in Brooklyn during the Depression and the lives of those I help in rural Nicaraguan villages.

Today, I find myself reflecting on my development as an individual and as a student, realizing that my Minga has humbled me. She has mentored me throughout my life with her serious advice and nurtured me through daily signs of support, such as her knocking on her ceiling (my floor) with a broom handle every morning to wake me up or her insistence on packing me a sandwich and a half with my lunch every day. Minga is a major influence in my life, and as I continue to pursue my interests in the academic world and beyond, I strive to be some type of "Minga" for others. Luckily, my initial inability to say "Grandma" hasn't held me back.

COMMENTARY

In this essay, the author reflects on his Polish grandmother—whom he calls "Minga"—and the tremendous influence she has had on various aspects of his outlook and development. By opening with an anecdote explaining his grandmother's nickname, he eases the reader into the story. Using his grandmother's story and personality as the essay's backdrop, he is able to discuss his past challenges and current goals without sounding self-absorbed. Using choice details, he paints a vivid and well-rounded picture of his role model. Minga loves cooking and Bingo; she also comes from a large, poor family in Depression-era New York. We know that Minga is inquisitive, skilled at poker, and unafraid to speak her mind. These details add charm and humor, and prevent his description of Minga from veering into hagiographic territory, a common pitfall in essays about older family members.

The author regularly presents the essay's more commonplace elements in a compelling way. "God never closes a door without opening a window" is not an uncommon saying, but he takes the metaphor and runs with it ("I've always found windows large enough to squeeze through") in discussing his own personal hardships. Note how in just one sentence he elegantly incorporates his mother's illness, his parents' divorce, and his school transfer without disrupting the essay.

His first mention of Nicaragua, however, is abrupt and somewhat confusing. Similarly, his grandmother's living situation is never quite explained. He mentions in the second paragraph that he "spent part of every weekend at her house," but in the conclusion he includes details that would suggest he lived with her (she wakes him up each morning, routinely packs his lunch). These particulars are charming and evocative, but it's difficult to fully appreciate them

V. Through Their Eyes: Finding Yourself in Others

when they're not situated properly. Overall, the author's personal and genuine approach throughout allows him to honor his grandmother and to express deeply held beliefs, thereby outweighing his occasional reliance on platitude.

—Jessica Henderson

PHILLIP ZHANG—"THE JOURNEY"

In the rural Chinese village where my father spent his adolescence, people believed that upon a man's death, he must collect all the footprints he has ever laid before being allowed to enter heaven. The villagers concluded that it therefore must be best not to venture far from home, and so they allowed the myth to bind them to their simple, everyday lives. My father saw things differently.

The son of a Shanghai doctor, my father grew up with dreams of studying and, later, working in a university for the benefit of society. But when that society, in the chaos of the Cultural Revolution, seemingly betrayed him by shutting down its universities and shipping him off into the countryside to "learn from the peasants," he was forced to reconsider his options. Separated from his family and without even a middle-school education, he remained hopeful, but uncertain, about his future. He began to learn on his own, believing that knowledge would serve him well regardless of his surroundings.

Ten years later at the end of the Cultural Revolution, my father took the national college entrance examination, competing with tens of millions of high school graduates for a limited number of places in the newly reopened schools. Remarkably, he received one of the highest scores on the examination and was admitted to Peking University, the nation's most prestigious institution. Later, he realized his dreams of studying neuroscience abroad and becoming a professor in the United States.

Although I have never lived in China, or in a rural farming village, I draw daily inspiration from my father's stories. He has bestowed in me a deep appreciation for life, a love of learning, and the courage to pursue my dreams. I have learned that there is no one "stairway" to heaven—we make our own path.

I keep this in mind as I prepare for the day when I, too, must venture away from the comfort of my own "village." While my father struggled to obtain opportunities to succeed, I endeavor to make full use of those that have been offered to me. Constantly striving to improve myself and my surroundings, I take the high road and encourage those around me to do so as well.

Growing up, I heard many stories about my father's life in the village. Now, I have stories of my own to share with him. Whether they are about the latest issue of the school newspaper, a successful chamber music performance, or this year's literary magazine theme, they always bring a smile to his face.

One day I hope to visit my father's old village. It is a long way from home, and I would leave many footprints along the way. But perhaps the real meaning of the villagers' parable is simply that we must all review and take responsibility for our deeds here on Earth—a theme of universal importance despite its humble origins in a rural Chinese village. When the time comes to collect my footprints, I hope to have left some lasting, positive impression on the lives of others.

Then, the journey will have been worth it.

COMMENTARY

The main strengths of this applicant's essay lie in the first half. Contrasting the mind-set of the villagers with his father's—and by extension his own—is an effective way to convey the applicant's sense of adventure and courage. It also cleverly grabs the reader's interest and makes him or her want to learn more. Another strength is the inclusion of the story of the author's father's struggle for success.

Though the tale is simple and compelling, it does not convey the applicant's own ambition loudly enough. The latter part of the essay could be improved by driving home this point. The applicant's assertion that he takes the high road and encourages others comes off as a little self-congratulatory. As that sentence comes right after the statement about taking advantage of opportunities, it might serve the applicant better to give more specific examples of the opportunities he has pursued.

One challenge that comes with this type of essay, which includes so much about another person's life, is the danger of conveying very little about the applicant. It might have served the author better to use a larger portion of the latter half of the essay to share more about himself through relating his life to his father's. Devoting more time to communicating information about how the applicant shares the virtues he admires in his father would have made for more illuminating prose.

—Anita Hofschneider

Giacomo Bagarella—"Gli Strati della Storia (The Layers of History)"

This essay is structured on the form of N. Scott Momaday's *The Way to Rainy Mountain*. There are three distinct parts: the sacred, the secular, and the private. In other words, oral history, linear history, and experiential history, respectively. The last piece connects a significant artifact from a previous generation with the present.

> *Odysseus the Astute was weary after ten years of war and ten more of exhausting travels. One quiet morning, he awoke ashore on his beautiful Ithaca, washed up on the familiar sand by the sea of Destiny. There, however, he learned that his enemies had been long since planning a marriage to his wife, the graceful Penelope, in order to lie with her in his bed of living wood. A bed which he himself had carved, a bed whose usurpation would mean the vanquishing of the rightful Ithacan dynasty. Odysseus furtively organized a plan; soon all of the suitors fell under his mighty blade and arrows, which had slain many an enemy before. He then took back what was his by birthright, and led a peaceful existence with his beloved wife and brave son, who would succeed upon his father's death to the throne of Ithaca.*

On September 3, 1943, Fascist Italy signed an armistice with the Allies. Soon after, the country was taken over by German forces crossing the Alps and by those already present on the peninsula. All Italian soldiers who had fought for their country on various fronts, including the African one, had been left to themselves. These veterans were dispersed all over the Mediterranean and in the middle of a terrible situation. Faced with violent Nazi reprisals, such as the one on the Greek island of Kefalonia, these men had to decide where they stood. Would they keep on fighting for the Fascist regime, remain neutral and withdraw from the conflict, or join the partisans and British and American forces to free their homeland from the Germans?

My paternal grandfather, Rodolfo Bagarella, was among these thousands of war-weary soldiers. He had piloted tanks in the highlands of Eritrea between 1936 and 1940, and spent the years between 1940 and 1943 maneuvering the steel machines in the sandy plains of Libya. Forced back across the Mediterranean by the Allied advance, he defended Sicily and Southern Italy until Italy's capitulation. Resolved that his fight for the wrong side had ended, he struggled his way back home to Vicenza by foot. He returned to his wife after having been gone for nearly ten years of military service, but his troubles were not yet over. He had to work to provide for his kin, and he also had to hide from German soldiers. They would have executed him as a "deserter" if they had caught him. This lasted until April 1945, when the Nazis were finally driven out of Italy. When Nonno Rodolfo died in an accident on his job in the family windmill in 1953, he left a widow and my six-year-old father, alone in post–World War II Italy, to fend for themselves and rebuild their lives amidst a ravaged country.

In the winter of 2004, during the Christmas holidays, I visited my grandfather's grave with my grandmother, father, and mother, cleaning it and breaking the ice to remember a man who had come back from distant lands and suffered to make his country ours again.

I know Nonno Rodolfo from two pictures. One of them is his wedding picture. The other is shot in Africa, and my grandfather is smiling with his tank crew and a young African child. I look up to this man, who in times of war and discrimination could show such a soothing smile and hug a kid who would have been set aside for the color of his skin, both in Europe and America. My grandfather never had the chance to tell me about his life, his opinions; he never had the opportunity to hold me on his lap and instruct me on how to grow up. But when I look at that picture, I think that no matter how much evil there is in the world, we can always hold goodness within ourselves and spread it to the people closest to us. I try to follow the feeling this old picture gives me, try to be like my grandfather in actions and thought. Luckily for everyone today, our times are much different from those he lived in. This is not an excuse, however, not to learn from the past. It has already repeated itself too many times, but if we all cherish the good our ancestors left us, then maybe the future will indeed be brighter.

COMMENTARY

The formal structure of this essay makes it a daring one. The introductory allusion to Momaday's novel is certainly a unique opening; however, it seems to be lost on those who haven't read the work, and the mere act of beginning the essay with a structural outline comes across as slightly formulaic for a personal statement. Indeed, the background information is necessary for anyone who has not read the work, but the space devoted to illuminating the novel more than the individual in question is a real gamble.

That said, the essay is most successful when the author takes a personalized approach. The vivid detail and striking storytelling abilities manifested in the fourth and fifth paragraphs effectively draw the reader's attention to the deeper story being told in the essay. Writing an essay about the importance of a family member and the values that he or she instilled is a commonplace topic, and one runs the risk of boring an admissions officer simply by virtue of that fact. The author avoids that pitfall, however, by writing not about the lessons he learned from his elder, but rather the lack thereof. By flipping the convention on its head, he forces readers to ponder what their own elders might have taught them had they had the chance, and shows his ability to draw meaning from complex problems and issues with ease.

—Marc Steinberg

Lisa Yao—"Untitled"

Eight-year-old girls are made in pairs. In a childhood game of "House," it takes the bare minimum of two to script out a family. When one girl earns a weekend trip to the barn, she finds a way to bring her counterpart along. Michelle and I were two peas in a pod.

When Michelle got "sick," my natural solution was to bring our playdates to her—even to the sterile confines of a hospital ward. In my third-grade vocabulary, "sick" encompassed anything from a cough to fevers to now the four-syllable condition, "leu-ke-mi-a." As I soon discovered, however, leukemia did not follow the usual course of illnesses, and our games soon lost their boisterous appeal. "House" was reduced to board games when her nosebleeds became too frequent, and later to garden strolls on the roof of Stanford's Children's Hospital. But even those had to end.

Michelle changed with my every visit. Physically, chemotherapy depleted her body, and all I saw was the void on her head that had once been covered with neat braids. The happy girl who once drew me into a pretend world of princesses and royalty took on an unfamiliar lethargy. That confused me. How come medicine couldn't kill the germs in her blood disease? Why wasn't I getting sick? And why didn't the doctors make my best friend better?

Even during my last visits, death still seemed like a sad story meant to exist only in the headlines of my morning newspaper. Our eyes were on the future as we made plans to go to the same high school and to one day buy houses on the same block. I vowed that when her hair grew back, we would even get matching haircuts. But I never had a chance to carry out my promise.

Michelle left much too soon, but my friendship with her shaped my view of time. I constantly remind myself of the transience of my high-school hours spent celebrating victorious sports games, studying for tests, and dancing to music. And yet, although ephemeral, my limited time still provides many opportunities to make enduring contributions. Ultimately, my visits to Michelle bore no healing power, but her fleeting smiles, forever preserved in my memories, were enough to influence the path that I would set for myself and the attitude with which I would face life.

I know that I will cross paths with many people in situations like Michelle's; I look to my experience in college as a way to prepare for these greater responsibilities. Instead of playing the role of a girlfriend, I will strive to combat the limitations of modern medicine by delving into the biological sciences. With the complexity of today's changing illnesses, the innovations in science cannot come fast enough. A cure may not yet exist for Michelle's affliction, but my friendship with her has taught me that there are infinitely many ways to bring hope to the critically ill and to ease their suffering.

I remember standing stoic and dry-eyed as I delivered Michelle's eulogy to somber pews of friends and relatives, unable to absorb the reality of losing a best friend. The thought of death and unsolvable mysteries still scares me. To an eight-year-old, hospitals seemed like a magical place where germs disappeared, but I now understand that doctors do not have all the solutions. Behind the scenes, hospitals are merely a joint effort by compassionate citizens using the means of the time to conquer big-worded diseases. Michelle found comfort in my companionship, but even that failed to prolong her body clock. The only way to keep a clock going is through an understanding of its function, and that is one thing that intrigues me about biology: the way it illuminates the underlying functions of life's phenomena. Whereas I was bound to the sidelines during Michelle's fight, there is a role I can play now. The opportunities to lend a hand are many, but whether through a career in medicine, research, or journalism, I hope to leave my fingerprint in the biological world and in the lives of the people I encounter.

COMMENTARY

The death of a friend or family member is a tempting subject for a personal statement, as it is an obvious source of rich emotion for a writer, but it can be difficult to pull off for these purposes. No matter how meaningful the event is to the applicant, admissions officers—who use the personal statements to learn more about the individual—may not be able to glean any more from grief-ridden essays than that emotion.

This essay takes this challenge and handles it well, turning a story about the passing of a dear childhood friend into a way to explain the applicant's motivation for studying medicine, a career path to which many applicants aspire. Using the personal statement to differentiate herself from others with similar academic and career goals is wise, especially given that the essay is effective.

The essay's subject of death is compelling, and it works best because it serves only as a backdrop to the story of the applicant herself—the applicant's struggle with death and her discovery of medicine as a life ambition is the central message that is conveyed.

The writer does not spend too much time describing her friend's personality or experiences, instead focusing on her own experiences, struggles, and growth, and the conclusions she draws indicate an admirable level of maturity and commitment to her goals. The discussion of science in the latter part of the essay also helps balance the sentimentality of a child's grief, and it helps achieve a detachment that further indicates maturity and gives important insight into the applicant's academic passions. However, there is

50 Successful Harvard Application Essays

always a danger in changing tone too drastically, and the applicant toes the line between a smooth and an awkward transition.

From the short introduction that aptly sets the scene, to the long conclusion that explains the applicant's love for biology, the essay has a smooth flow that comes from its consistency of content and writing style. One criticism might be that the essay runs a little long, but because each sentence is thoughtful and thought-provoking, the length does not detract too much from the whole. That said, adhering to word limits is important, as admissions officers have limited time.

—Anita Hofschneider

190

Xi Yu—"Mother"

My cheek pressed against the cold glass. I allowed my eyes to lose focus as I lazily watched the white line delineating the road run past.

My mother's voice broke the trance. I jerked from the passenger window.

"Have you finished the paper yet?" she asked.

Whenever you make toast, some slices burn more than others. If my family did eat toast for breakfast, Mother would always have the burnt one.

Perhaps it is the mother's job to care for everyone in the home. Mother nags my brother to do his schoolwork. My father enjoys her cooking after a long day. Mother supports most of my endeavors.

The chill air tickles my damp face as I trudge back to our team campsite. After eighteen hours of lapping the track to fund the cure, I am exhausted. I squint against the rising sun to watch my mother, in her tirelessness, drop the last batch of egg rolls into the sizzling oil.

The language barrier between Mother and me is enough to create our occasional vicissitudes. It frustrates me when she creates confusion since she cannot speak English well. Although I am fluent in Chinese, my vocabulary is limited to colloquial discourse, unusable for intellectual thought.

Such is the case when I try to explain sarcasm to Mother, a device, which I have learned, the Chinese rarely use. In our heated confrontations over why I should not be staying up so late to work on the school newspaper, I use it lavishly.

"I stay up late because the pages are so perfect, Mom," I would say to her in defiance.

"Well, then you shouldn't need to, right?" she would reply.

I feel the sun's shy warmth as I zip up the last sleeping bag. All my team members have left. I turn in my Team Captain's box as my eyes close; I feel I can instantaneously fall to the grass and sleep. My mother pushes the dolly containing the propane tank, tents, cooler, and chairs from my hands, and tells me to wait in the car.

I have learned that cancer is a language that both Mother and I can understand. Her sister was recently touched by cancer, and her brother died from it before I was born. Hence, she willingly chaperones the hardest shift every year at our school's Relay For Life. She is the one who stays at our booth to sell the egg rolls, helping us raise money. In the morning, when energy is at its worst, Mother pushes us to move out before we collapse.

I only begin to appreciate Mother's kindness, and I must learn to understand her. She has taught me the value of hard work, and she has taught me what it means to care. More importantly, she has taught me how to be. I hope to do for the world what Mother has done for me.

I looked at her, startled. The school track disappeared from my peripheral.

"I mean, aren't you going to finish the paper once we get home? You can't possibly be tired now, right?" my mother asked.

I stared at her, then relaxed, and smiled to myself.

"Did I do it right?" she asked. "Was that it?"

I closed my eyes. I understood.

Yes, Mother, you did. You did.

V. Through Their Eyes: Finding Yourself in Others

COMMENTARY

Writing about a family member who has had a significant impact on your life can be a risky move, as you can expect countless application essays on this topic, but when done well, it can be very memorable. The key to a successful essay is to keep it real—don't turn your role model into a martyr, don't present the relationship as flawless and overbearingly positive. This essay succeeds in that it does not attempt to hide the points of tension bound to come up in any parent-child relationship, while painting a realistic portrait of the author's mother.

It is not necessary to structure your college application essay in a unique way, and you run a risk of confusing admissions officers, who will already have skimmed countless essays before picking up yours. The middle section of this essay features numerous snippets into the author's relationship with her mother, but the lack of transitions contributes to a somewhat scattered section. Although providing examples can help the reader better understand the relationship, make sure that the reader can follow you every time you jump to different flashbacks.

The essay's strength lies in its honest voice, as the author recognizes that despite her grievances, there is much to appreciate in her mother. Underneath the occasional nagging and stilted English, there is much to learn from her mother, and the author recognizes that she has only begun to understand her relationship.

—June Wu

MEICHENG SHI—"DELVE!"

"Delve!" my English teacher exclaimed, fingers plowing through the air, as if yanking a motif out of the text. Her words were spoken with such passion that it made me want to reach deeper, too, to delve into the depths of the literary work and dig out the treasures that were buried beneath the plot, in between the lines. I wouldn't call her an imposing character; the atmosphere of the class was laid-back and almost relaxing, except that we were discussing literary philosophies, which hovered above my head like a foggy blanket.

Yet, she challenged us to bounce the ball of thought back and forth, penetrating the cloud of ideas by using each other to build up our own discoveries. Every once in a while, she would reach out and grab part of the web being formed, raising it up, and questioning it. "Pursue this," she would state, her words tinged with the hint of some secret theme to be revealed. Like dogs eager to catch the ball, we would go where she pointed, only to discover that the thoughts we strung together were our own, something of our own creation.

Occasionally, she would grace us with her artistic abilities by scrawling stick figures on the board, weighed down by disproportional crowns and stuck living in castles half their size. The protagonist of the bildungsroman would undertake a journey of epic proportion, only to be shrunk by her white board marker to a bare segment from point A to B. But the simplistic lines and anorexic heroes only magnified the ideas that she drew into the classroom, into our minds. Skeletal depictions of the journey left more room for words, thoughts, and ideas about the journey itself; the architecturally infeasible castle illuminated our understanding of the inherent difference between the murdered king's leadership style and that of Claudius in *Hamlet*.

So enchanted were we that we accepted any assignment in class, only to return home and find out we had agreed without complaint to a twelve-page research paper. Her outrageously funny stories made everyone, including herself, burst out in a cackle of laughter, while her easygoing personality convinced us that the workload was easygoing as well; it made a daunting task seem like child's play. I had always been taught to write a hamburger: bread for the introduction and the conclusion, with cheese, lettuce, and meat as the three main points. But she resisted that traditional five-paragraph essay. "Your thesis sets the essay up," she assured us with a smile. All we had to do was interpret the text, to keep the thesis rooted in the text. Her concluding comment was always a warning to stay away from SparkNotes. "You don't need it," she repeated before every essay.

And we didn't need it. We had her.

COMMENTARY

A testament to her English teacher's influences, the author's essay shows true literary aptitude. While it focuses mainly on the teacher, it indirectly sheds light on the author's personality. The subtle and humorous depiction of her English teacher's stick-figure drawings reflects the narrator's vivid imagination. The repetition and evolution of words and images throughout the essay display the author's creative abilities. The reader is left knowing that this is a young woman with real literary talents.

The essay is also heavy on specific lessons learned in English class. While some of these details help shape the overall structure of the essay, additional information is unnecessary and distracts the reader from the writer herself. This is a personal statement, not a recital of everything your teacher has told you in the classroom. Be careful of focusing too much on the abstract—be as concrete as you can when writing your admissions essay.

This piece would benefit from a section that details how the teacher influenced the writer beyond the classroom. For example, has her love of literature led to an involvement with a school publication? Did her creative abilities garner any local or national writing awards? These are all memorable details that will bolster the application as a whole.

—Manning Ding

Saieed Hasnoo—"A Ride Through the Field"

Sometimes I wake up in the morning and hope to see my grandpa waiting there once again to ride along the sugarcane fields. I can smell the distinctive aroma of curry and *dhal*, hear the radio playing classic calypso tunes, and even see my grandpa standing beside my bed in his favorite red polo shirt and brown khaki pants. He pulls the covers off the bed, and I leap out of bed hurriedly. Although my dad is hard at work fixing the car with my brother, my grandpa is never too busy to go for a ride with his favorite grandson. He dismounts the bikes from under the shed and brings them to the front of the yard, where we pack up our lunches and set off into the early morning. My grandpa was a great man.

Although I have no recollection of what exactly he looked like, no pictures of us together, and no intimate letters, I will always remember our weekend rides through the sugarcane fields in Trinidad. It was these journeys that taught me the most important thing in life, although I would not realize it until years later.

My father never really understood what was so special about our trips. We would ride slowly through the gravel roads, past the plantations and down deep into the forest groves where there hardly existed another soul. For my grandpa, the most special part of our nearly daylong voyage came at dusk when we would sit near the Hillsboro Lake and watch the scarlet ibises, beautiful birds that made their nests near the bank of the lake. We would sit there for literally hours, speaking ever so scarcely, just enjoying the company of each other, and the birds. I once asked him, "How come the birds always come back, papa? I mean, to the same place." After a pensive moment, he replied, "That's where they build their nests. That's where their heart is. Never forget that."

That is one thing I never did.

Sometimes I feel that the most difficult thing was letting go of my grandpa in that airport. He was sobbing, for reasons I could have not possibly understood at the age of eight. My father assured me that this was the most important decision that we as a family had made and that America would change our lives for the better. We were moving on to a brand-new world. It seems as if my grandpa had known something that day, something I wish I had known sooner.

At first, I didn't know how to react to his death. In my mind, he was invincible—I couldn't even manage to cry. The day that I found out I simply sat in my room, looking out the window, and wondering if my grandpa was looking down at me. It was the first day that I had been absent from school in over ten years.

It was that day that I realized what made my grandpa weep. Up until that point, what my father had predicted was true. America had changed us, it had changed us all. My father had left home, my mother was constantly working, and I virtually never saw my brother. My family was falling apart. However, out of this circumstance came hope. My grandpa had made me a stronger man and made me understand the importance of family. It was my goal—rather my obligation—to fulfill the tacit promise that I made to him that day.

Although a seemingly trivial task, approaching my father was one of the hardest things I have ever done. Listening to the words of my grandpa, I related to him the emotions that had been pent up inside of me for too long. I told him about my fears of our separation, my longing for the rekindling of our relationship, and the fleeting time that we had left to accomplish these rather impossible aspirations. As we sat together, embracing the tears that began to heal our wounds, he finally understood what was so special about my relationship with my beloved grandpa, and so did I.

COMMENTARY

In this artful essay, the applicant crafts a telling narrative about his immigration to the United States and the subsequent unraveling of his family, as well as its reunion. He uses vivid sensory details—the smell of curry, the sound of calypso music, his grandfather's outfit, and scarlet ibises—to personalize the story. This essay is successful because it seamlessly integrates two tenets of the college essay: anecdotes and understanding. The writer highlights the origins of his bond with his grandfather by describing their habitual bike rides. Indeed, the writer creates the sense of a home.

The applicant zooms in on subtle, yet poignant moments to craft his narrative. In his essay, the author is making the case that he will heed his grandfather's advice and will remain loyal to his entire family. By minimizing the trauma in his life and celebrating the memory of his grandfather, the writer shows that he has focused on the positive legacy of his grandfather to empower himself.

Though this essay is exceptionally strong, the applicant could have made the timeline of his life in America more explicit. We jump from the sorrowful good-bye at the airport in Trinidad to at least a decade later when the writer learns of his grandfather's death. A transition sentence between these events might have helped orient the reader. However, all in all, this is a deeply introspective piece that catapults the clichéd essay topic of the totem grandparent into a moving lesson about family obligation and unforeseen difficulties of immigration.

—Laura Mirviss

Sam Novey—"Untitled"

The cha-cha slide was pumping from speakers on both sides of the room. Frantically, I was trying to keep up with the song's instructions. I slid to the left. I slid to the right. I took four hops. I even successfully cha-chaed. But when the lyrics asked, "Can you bring it to the top like you never never stop?" my answer was a resounding "No."

It was a pretty typical Bar Mitzvah party. Adults were trying to be heard over the DJ's loud music and middle-schoolers were looking awkward on the dance floor. But for me, this party was different. It was being held at the Cross Keys Radisson Hotel, where I had worked as a busboy over the summer. The man circulating the room with a tray of hors d'oeuvres was Jesse, my former co-worker. The busboy collecting used plates was Anthony, who had, on my first day, given me a patient tutorial on napkin folding.

Over the summer, we all had spent many nights commiserating about the mess kids left behind after parties. And now, as I looked around the room, I thought of how much work this would make for Armand, the Ukrainian dishwasher. When business was slow over the summer, I had helped him with his English in the back of the restaurant. Jesse and I chatted, but it was weird. Despite our previous friendships, it was awkward talking with my former co-workers. Tonight, I was one of those messy kids after whom I had so often cleaned up.

We have an unfortunate tendency to separate people into "us" and "them." That night at the Radisson, the dividing line was class. What made me a guest putting food on a plate rather than a

V. Through Their Eyes: Finding Yourself in Others

busboy scraping it off was nothing more than the circumstances of my birth.

Because I had been on both sides of the kitchen door, the distinction between "us" and "them" suddenly became blurred.

Months later, I felt this same self-consciousness during my internship at KIPP DC: AIM Academy. KIPP is a public-charter middle school in southeast Washington, D.C. It strives to place disadvantaged kids on a college preparatory track before they get too far behind in southeast D.C.'s underfunded public schools. I had started out in July just trying to finish my community-service hours but ended up staying on until the end of the summer.

Only one week into KIPP's mandatory summer school, LeeShawn Smith was the second student to be expelled. As the office intern, I had seen a lot of ten-year-old LeeShawn that week.

Smart and creative, but not interested in school, he was constantly being sent to the office for something. More than anything, he was averse to following rules and immune to intimidation by adults. After five days of refusing to respond to his teachers, Lee-Shawn was thrown out.

That afternoon, the principal asked me to walk LeeShawn to the bus stop. As we sat side by side waiting for the A4, I recognized in LeeShawn many aspects of myself as a ten-year-old: bored by school and disrespectful to teachers, but pretty smart and not without potential. Thinking of LeeShawn's poor behavior, I recalled my former career as a middle-school subversive. There was the time in sixth grade when I dumped a trash can on a girl's head.

And then there was the more recent incident in eleventh grade when I hit my Spanish teacher in the face with a hockey puck and then pretended it wasn't me.

Yet, while I had been given countless opportunities to mess up and learn from my mistakes, LeeShawn, in a single week of bad behavior, had just blown his chance at early placement on a college preparatory track. At LeeShawn's neighborhood high school, only 7 percent of students can read "proficiently." Less than 8 percent of students go to college. Three-quarters never even graduate from high school. At my private preparatory high school, 100 percent of students graduate from high school, and 100 percent go to college.

When we walk across the stage to receive our diplomas this June, my classmates and I will have a lot to be proud of. Year after year, we have tucked in our shirts, turned in our homework, and hustled on the athletic field. But while we should be proud of our hard work, we should also be aware of what we have not personally earned. Many of us were born into comfortable homes, to parents who care deeply about our education. We have played our cards well, but we have been dealt a very good hand.

In his book, *A Hope in the Unseen*, Ron Suskind writes of what he calls "generational succession: a child's footsteps following their [parents], steps on a path that leads to prosperity's table and a saved seat right next to Mom and Dad." It is easy to feel like we are entitled to our future college degrees and lucrative careers.

But it is hard to acknowledge that much of our success is a result of what we have been given rather than what we have earned.

Separating people into "us" and "them" can lead to a sense of entitlement. It is human nature to think of the people around you as "us." If all of your friends have personal cell phones, cars, and the opportunity for a good education, then those who do not fit that profile soon become "them." They are out of sight and out of mind. The man circulating around the room with a tray of hors d'oeuvres is not a person trying to make ends meet with a minimum wage job, but just another guy in a bow tie who maybe should have worked a little harder. By identifying with "us," you dehumanize "them." It makes it easier to justify unfairly concentrated resources. This vicious cycle perpetuates inequality.

In 2031, my class will return to Baltimore for our twenty-fifth reunion. We will mill around in our polo shirts and khakis, with bald spots in place of formerly robust lax mullets. It will not be long before we are chuckling over the hijinks of our youth. We will recall the cultivation of the maggot-infested sandwich in the junior locker room and the airborne couch of 2004. But being able to reminisce and laugh about our mischievous years is a luxury. We have been allowed to mess up, learn from our mistakes, and get back on our feet.

We have a safety net of social and educational resources that will keep us on track to graduate high school, go to college, and land a good job while we sort through the growing pains of adolescence.

In many respects, it is to my high school's credit that among its graduates there is such extensive educational and professional success, but that success is only made possible by enormous resources. We should be ashamed to live in a society that has so many resources for some of its members, yet so few for others. Where is the safety net to catch LeeShawn? It is only by opening our eyes to the way we have benefitted from an unfair system that we can become part of the solution.

COMMENTARY

College applicants come from all types of backgrounds. The writer of this essay does not pretend to have overcome great struggles and acknowledges that he grew up in a stable, privileged environment.

He recounts experiences that helped him realize that not all people come from similarly fortunate circumstances, and his essay is an honest and candid discussion of the class inequalities that exist in our society. He is thankful for his own background and shows great care and compassion for those without the same opportunities. Through this essay, the writer shows that he is concerned about societal inequality, and will likely work to effect social change in the future. Like many of the successful essays in this book, the piece begins with a vivid and humorous anecdote (dancing at a Bar Mitzvah party), and moves forward in a succession of scenes including LeeShawn and a hypothetical high school reunion.

What might resonate about this essay with an admissions officer? "Diversity" is, with good reason, the watchword of the day in universities all over the country. However, admissions recognizes that simply admitting people of different backgrounds isn't sufficient to reap the benefits that diversity is supposed to entail. Rather, it is necessary to admit people who not only have distinctive upbringings and experiences, but also demonstrate a capacity to be receptive to and learn from their counterparts and the world around them. This essay shows a keen ability to learn from others and makes its writer a good fit for a university environment. When you are writing, think about how you can convince the readers that you are somebody who will take advantage of the lessons your extraordinary classmates will have to offer.

This is an incredibly long essay, and the writer bounces through a multitude of different situations and topics in these 1,200 words. While his message runs throughout his different sections, he could have conveyed the same ideas in a much more concise form. It's best not to test the patience of an admissions officer with a piece this long if it can be avoided. Stick to the 600- or 700-word range (two pages, double-spaced) if possible.

V. Through Their Eyes: Finding Yourself in Others

Despite its length, the reader leaves this essay with a clear view of who the author is—not only a privileged prep school student, but also a sympathetic individual passionate about social change.

—Lauren Kiel

Edith Chan—"My Mother"

I was eight years old. My mother was tucking me into bed one night when she gently asked me a question I would never forget. "Sweetie, my company wants to promote me but needs me to move to Japan to work. This is like your teacher telling you that you've done well and allowing you to skip a grade, but you'll have to leave your friends behind. Would you say yes to your teacher?" She gave me a hug and asked me to think about it. Puzzled, the question kept me wondering for the rest of the night. I had said "yes" but for the first time, I realized the tough decisions adults had to make.

Soon afterward, my mother was assigned to Japan. She would call us every day. For almost four years, no matter where she was, this discipline of hers never faltered. I always looked forward to this daily routine, and every evening I would place myself right next to the telephone, books in my hands, and wait for the phone to ring. I'd ramble on about every detail—from the squabbles with my brother to my excitement for the school's swim meet. A phone call, however, could never substitute for her presence and it was difficult not to feel lonely at times.

During my fourth-grade Christmas break, we flew to Tokyo to visit her—the first time since she had moved there. Looking at her large apartment, unadorned and empty, I became aware of how lonely my mother must have been in Japan herself. Separated from family and living in a foreign land with a language she did not speak, she must have felt vulnerable, too. It was then that I started to appreciate the tough choices she had to make on balancing family and work. Faced with difficult decisions, she used to tell me, very

V. Through Their Eyes: Finding Yourself in Others

often you would not know whether you made the right choice, but you could always make the best out of the situation, with passion and a positive attitude. Keep smiling, she would often say.

Back in Hong Kong, I reminded myself that what my mother could do, I could, too. If she managed to live in Tokyo all by herself, I, too, could learn to be independent. I learned how to take care of myself, to plan my time, and to set high but achievable goals. Over the phone, I could always identify the determination I admire in her voice, and in her stories about work and Japan, her enthusiasm to work, her adventurous spirit, and her sense of humor.

My mother continues to do well at work and is now back with us. Sometimes, I wonder if she knows how much the experience has really taught me. That self-sufficiency is learned; that persistence is developed; and that sacrifices pay off in the end. The separation between us has really been a blessing in disguise.

COMMENTARY

In this essay the author effectively uses her relationship with her mother to explain how her mother's career decisions affected her character. This essay could have easily come across as a cliché—she is writing about her mother after all—but because she presents her mother as a dynamic character, she avoids creating a static, boring essay.

The use of her mother's quote at the beginning of the essay helps showcase her mother's character traits, which will be key to explaining the author's own personality. The writer goes on to explain the hardship she experienced as a result of her mother living in Japan, but it should be noted that this is a secondary element of the essay. Clearly, she has experienced a deal of hardship as a result of living away from her mother, but hardship in isolation is fairly uninteresting. Callous though it may sound, admissions officers will be much more interested in hearing how one grew as a person as a result of the hardship one has experienced than the fact that one has experienced pain at some point in one's life.

During the last three paragraphs, the writer elaborates on her relationship with her mother and how distance has affected and, most important, strengthened her. The reader understands that the mother faced a difficult decision in moving to Japan, but that she was able to make the best of her move, an attitude that the author understands and has internalized. She explains that the ability to overcome difficulty she learned from her mother has helped her reach her own goals.

The most important take-away from this essay is to remember that while painful experiences in life make for powerful essay topics, that does not mean that the essay should focus on the pain itself. Rather, one should explain how one has grown as a result of the experience.

—Elias Groll